D1522303

What the River Means

Emerging Writers in Creative Nonfiction

WHAT
THE
RIVER
MEANS

ELIZABETH HODGES

EMERGING WRITERS IN CREATIVE NONFICTION

DUQUESNE
UNIVERSITY PRESS
PITTSBURGH, PA

Published by
Duquesne University Press
600 Forbes Avenue
Pittsburgh, Pennsylvania 15282

Library of Congress Cataloging-in-Publication Data

Hodges, Elizabeth, 1953–
        What the river means / by Elizabeth Hodges.
        p.   cm. — (Emerging writers in creative nonfiction)
        ISBN 0–8207–0294–3 (acid-free paper)
        1. Hodges, Elizabeth, 1953– 2. Pennsylvania — Biography. 3.
Maryland — Biography.   4. Seven River (Md.) — Description and travel.
I. Title.   II. Series.
        CT275.H628345 A3 1998
        974.8'043'092 — ddc21
        [B]
                                                                    98–40092
                                                                         CIP

Several chapters, in different versions, originally appeared in the following periodi-
cals: *Maryland English Journal*: "My Grandfather and the Fish"; *Creative Nonfiction*:
"Death by African Violet" and "Radio Wars, Closed Doors, When You're Out I
Check Your Drawers"; *Emrys Journal*: "Decapitating Crocuses"; *Sonora Review*: "Before
the Storm"; *Potomac Review*: a section of "Crossing with Deer, Providence Road."

"Do You Believe in Magic," by John Sebastian
© 1966 Trio Music Company, Inc., Alley Music Corp.
Copyright renewed. All rights reserved. Used by permission.

"Happy Together," by Gary Bonner, Alan Gordon
© 1966 Trio Music Company, Inc., Alley Music Corp.
Copyright renewed. All rights reserved. Used by permission.

"Goin' Out Of My Head," by Teddy Randazzo and Bobby Weinstein
© 1964 Songs of PolyGram International, Inc.
Copyright renewed. All rights reserved. Used by permission.

"This Diamond Ring," by Al Kooper and Irwin Levine
© 1964, 1965 Warner Bros. Publications
Copyright renewed. All rights reserved. Used by permission.

"These Boots Are Made for Walkin'," by Lee Hazlewood
© 1965 Criterion Music Corporation
Copyright renewed & assigned 1993 Criterion Music Corporation
Used by permission. International copyright secured.

Printed on acid-free paper.

In Memoriam

Kathleen Hodges Cabassa, 3–18–60 to 11–21–94

The truth: what is oblique. *A monk once asked Kao Tsu: "What is the unique and final work of truth?" . . . The master replied: "Yes."* I take this answer not as a vague prejudice in favor of general acquiescence as the philosophical secret of truth. I understand that the master, bizarrely opposing an adverb to a pronoun, yes to what, replies obliquely; he makes a deaf man's answer, of the same kind as he made to another monk who asked him: "All things are said to be reducible to the One; but to what is the One reducible?" And Kao Tsu replied: "When I was in the Ching district, I had a robe made for me which weighed seven kin."*

Roland Barthes,
A Lover's Discourse: Fragments

Contents

Thoughts and Thanks

Books start in many places. In one respect this book began in and around the Severn River in Maryland. I thank the people and good fortune which made it possible for me to spend the first fourteen and a half years of my life there. I am grateful, too, that those years fell during an era which was, in many ways, still innocent enough that children were allowed to range and explore.

This book began, in another way, when I was 28 and trying hard to tell the story of my grandfather and the fish. I tried to tell it as fiction, but its telling, at least for this writer, does not lend itself to that genre because the man in the boat in August of 1963 and, later, in my parents' bed, a guest in our home in 1973, ceased to be my grandfather when I fleshed him out, developing his character more fully than I ever knew that of the real man, trying to make him three-dimensional and authentic in that way that good fiction demands writers develop character. In truth, many of the people who have poured past me in my life, talking, acting, are people whom I can never really know except as they exist in my memories and the memories of the few around me who shared these people with me. And it is possible, always possible, even likely, that we each knew them differently.

I know that both of my sisters saw them and responded to, for example, our grandparents very differently than did I. Thus the people who tread through this book may not see themselves as I see them. That is their right, as being true to my memory of them is mine. Except for a few instances, I have changed names and smudged edges, and held back stories I might have told, out of respect for how people's lives have proceeded and in order to give anonymity, but there are no composite characters.

This book began a second time in 1993 on the island of Ocracoke off the coast of North Carolina, the place where I have come closest to reclaiming the love and freedom of salt water and tides and marshes and explorations with which I grew up. The ecologies of this island and the Severn are uncannily similar in spirit. I went to Ocracoke in late November of 1993 and stayed into early January of 1994, trying to reclaim myself as a writer for both professional and personal reasons. I thank the people of Ocracoke Realty who found for me a perfect and affordable haven in which to do my work. I thank the people whom I encountered daily, particularly those who work at the Variety Store and the post office and the South Point fish house on the harbor, who were open and kind to me during a time when their entire small community was healing from the "on" season and the thousands of tourists who had visited their island that summer. I thank, particularly, Candy Gaskill of Albert Styron's General Store, who, when this outsider strayed in, was always willing to share some time and conversation, to share her observations and wry wit.

But once the book had begun, I needed readers. And just as I found beautiful swimmers (crabs) in my youth, I found beautiful readers, critics, more than I can name here. I thank Jenny Bradner who read this book so thoroughly that she recites lines from it. Amongst my former graduate students, I thank Joanne Jensen, Anne Carle, Catherine Ruziack, John Sexton, Jamelle Wilson, Ellen Davies, Mary Lou Odom and Sunni McMillan. Amongst my colleagues, I thank Angier Brock Caudle and Leslie Shiel, gifted poets and essayists, both of whom thought I was writing a book before I, myself, was certain. I thank Bonnie Hall, Esther Floyd, Therese Kohl, Alex Fagan and Leila Christenbury for their faith and support, and Angie Koziara for her ear. I thank my colleague and reader, Jeff Lodge, with whom I share a love of prose and a love of birds. I thank my colleague Jim Kinney for a decade of consistent support, and my colleague Pat Perry who insisted that I name frankly and honestly the racism I was depicting, insisting that I keep learning to name. Most amongst my colleagues, I thank Michael Keller, a gifted poet and essayist, who called me back to the writing of non-fiction with his love for the genre and his recognition of my own love for it. I wonder if this book would exist at all had our paths not both led to the third floor of Hibbs Building in 1989, where we have walked since. I thank, too, my chair, Richard Fine, who has respected and supported this work outside of the field of composition studies.

Others: I thank my copyeditor, Sandra Boatwright, for her excellent advice and for reading the book I thought I had written. I thank those who have respected my writing enough to publish it, amongst them Susan Wadsworth-Booth of Duquesne University Press, Lee Gutkind of *Creative Nonfiction*, Eli Flam of *Potomac Review*, Cathleen Church of *Sonora Review*, Jeanne Halva-Neubauer of *The Emrys Journal*, and Judith Pula of *Maryland English Journal*.

And most, I thank my home team of readers: Dona Hickey of the University of Richmond who has, as my friend and weekly writing group (and I hers), read every piece in this book, and pieces not in it, carefully and caringly, more than once. I thank, too, my dear friend and most patient reader, Neil Henry, who has actually read this book more times through than I or anyone else and claims to have enjoyed it each time more than the last. Both Neil and Dona have given me some of the sagest readerly advice. And last, I thank my parents, Frances and Addison Hodges, who have also read the whole for me several times, helping me with history, filling in with fact, discussing possibilities, shedding some tears and keeping me from fiction. I thank them, too, for giving me to the river in the first place and helping me value the cords that bind.

1

Faces Pouring Past Me Talking

There's a widespread notion that children are open, that the truth about their inner selves just seeps out of them. That's all wrong. No one is more covert than a child, and no one has a greater need to be that way. It's a response to a world that's always using a can opener to open them up to see what's inside, wondering whether it ought to be replaced with a more useful sort of preserves.

Peter Hoag,
Smilla's Sense of Snow

He lifts from the water. Water beads on his shoulders. I see the water in balls heavy as planets, a billion beads of water as weighty as worlds, and he lifts them up on his back as he rises. He stands wet in the water. Each one bead is transparent, and each has a world, or the same world, light and alive and apparent inside the drop: it is all there ever could be, moving at once, past and future, and all the people. I can look into any sphere and see people stream past me, and cool my eyes with colors and the sight of the world in spectacle perishing ever, and ever renewed I do; I deepen into a drop and see all that time contains, all the faces and deeps of the worlds and all the earth's contents, every landscape and room, everything living or made or fashioned, all past and future stars, and especially faces, faces like the cells of everything, faces pouring past me talking, and going, and gone. And I am gone.

Annie Dillard,
Holy the Firm

My Grandfather and the Fish

The pike is a fierce and voracious fish, even devouring small waterfowl and mammals, and it puts up a strong fight when hooked.

— James Beard, *James Beard's Fish Cookery*

Pike will eat their young.

— Barry Lopez, "Yukon-Charley: The Shape of Wilderness"

Dawn, August 1963   Dog days on the Severn River: the water is bathtub warm and brown from an August of no rain and endless heat. The tides rise and fall in slow motion as if they rise and fall in vats of molasses. There are dead fish on the shore. The stinging nettles are big, and they come in white and pink, yellow and rose, purple. We kids are sure that the different colors actually sting with different severity. Adults do not agree, but we kids are right. When the nettles arrive, we usually just smear on vaseline and mineral oil and let their slick coating try and protect us. But this summer is extra bad. No one — not even the dogs — will go in the water, and that is serious surrender.

For several years, I have been going out with my grandfather in his boat most mornings when he goes fishing. He can't eat fish anymore, but the fire to catch them schedules his retirement. I am his tender. He had a problem with sunstroke (brought on by Old Crow bourbon) when I was seven, and since then I have gone out with him most days in case the sun gets to him again and he wouldn't be able to get himself home.

Early every morning I leave my house with a bacon and egg sandwich in my hand and cut across our back yard and a neighbor's to the road, to the beach hill, and down to the pier. My grandfather always leaves about the same time and drives down. He's always there waiting in his skiff when I arrive, and he always tells me I am late. I climb silently off the pier into the skiff, never suggesting that I ride with him. I like the walk alone through dew-damp grass in innocent morning light. Nor does he suggest I ride with him, and I never wonder why.

As my grandfather primes the engine, thumb thunking the black button on the greasy red gas tank, I inhale slowly the perfume of the diluted gasoline that radiates out from the five horse outboard in concentric rainbow circles on the brown glass surface of the motionless morning river. Then I watch the rainbow shatter into ripples of hues when he pulls the cord and the engine sputters to life. We back away from the pilings with a comforting growl and putt around the end of the pier to an area, just down river from the pier, where boats too large and deep to moor at the pier are moored at floating buoys, small empty barrels like beer kegs or red and orange spheres the size of beach balls, all chained to cement anchors. We tie the skiff to his buoy, pull up to his big boat with its many horsepower motors and clamber aboard. For me it is always a scramble. Every day I bark the same part of my left shin bone climbing the three feet up from the edge of the skiff into his fishing boat.

We fish all over, up river for yellow perch, down toward the bay for white perch, blues, croakers, spot. Nine miles down where the Severn meets the Chesapeake we troll out into the bay over oyster beds for rockfish, often pulling up toadfish, which Granddaddy pierces through the brain with a hunting knife and flings off the stern, slicing their bodies out over the water in an arc of red spray. One day, in silence, we skim across the river and down toward Annapolis, nibbling on the forbidden Danishes he always manages to have on board, him sipping from a thermos of coffee steaming with the scent of bourbon. We come abreast of a point, just after the next-to-last bridge, and turn right into a cove you wouldn't know is there, if you didn't know the river well. He calls to me over the engine to be ready to drop the anchor, and I am. When he says "Now," I drop it and read its rope with my palms as it skips along the bottom until it snags. Then we bait, cast, and sit to fish.

As usual, I have one rod and reel. He has three. I sit with mine in my hands, daydreaming as I stare off down its length. He sits watching his as they stretch from their rod holders on the deck of his boat. It is a perfect spot, over weeds just off a sandbar. The fish nibble. The lapping and swelling lull. The gentle water slaps the wood of the boat playfully where water and hull meet. Out on the river beyond the cove, engines of other boats hum steadily, near then away, remote and calming like the drone of cicadas in steaming, still summer. Near the far shore, a blue heron fishes along with us. A true angler, so still and silent. We watch for golf balls from the course above the point to zing out into the water. "Waste of money," my grandfather says. "Gone forever."

"Not necessarily," I think, knowing of a Nancy Drew mystery in which Nancy finds the golf ball clue in several feet of water. Sometimes, too, I kayak over here on my own and search the shore and shallows for balls for my father.

We are fishing for perch, white or yellow. For a while we catch them just right, not too fast, not too slow. The stringer of fish looks healthier and healthier each time we pull it from the water to add a fish. We've caught several good dinners here, and soon it will soon be time to go. My line starts out again and the pole begins to bend. I feel sharp hard tugs and uneven pauses. Hard. Almost too hard. I get excited. Granddaddy grabs the pole from me and pulls it back in a huge long-armed arc. Graceful. Whatever has the hook resists, then pauses. "It's an eel, Bets." He hands the pole back. "Don't bring an eel into the boat."

Eels. In this river they get as much as six, maybe seven feet long and two and a half, even three inches in diameter. They are like snakes only slimy. My dad and uncles like to eat them. Me, they just fascinate and scare. I have a hard time resisting the urge to catch them, maybe to get them on *my* turf, if only so I can study them hard.

If this *is* an eel, which I know for sure it isn't, it will be the biggest I have seen. I keep reeling and feeling the line and my grandfather keeps warning me about the consequences of bringing an eel into the boat. You can never completely wash an eel away. Where they touch a pier, a boat, they leave a sticky coating of green mucous vegetable scunge all over. You always know where an eel has been. And if you get a finger in its mouth, it is like your finger is caught in a pair of heavy relentless pliers. But I know this isn't an eel. My grandfather just won't listen. And I have to make sure, just a look.

Back and forth we go —

"It's not an eel."

"It's an *eel*, Bets."

"It's not an eel."

"It's an eel, Bets."

— till I see a shadowy shape rising sharply yet eerily from the murk and beginning to fight harder and harder. I call out, "It's a barracuda, Granddaddy." But my grandfather sits and ignores me. Doesn't budge. Doesn't look. Angry. He opens his newspaper between us like a curtain. "I need the net. I can't hardly hold this." He ignores me still. So I wrench the fish somehow up and into the boat.

It is a pike. Easily eight pounds. Maybe more. It throws those pounds around with a frenzy I am sure will land it out of the boat again. But my grandfather snaps to action, grabs the fish and yells "Line! Line!" I reel in some, not realizing he wants more line instead of less. He yells. My hook has pierced his thumb, past the barb. He wrenches it out and then, and then? Then he begins a steady and economical purging of the boat.

My rod goes first. He breaks the pole into four pieces and throws the handful of shiny shellacked brown sticks over the side in a bunch, punching the water. Then the cushions. Orange. Blue. Green. One by one in quick succession they fly low over the water, spinning like boomerangs, till they slap into a skid on the surface and skip like stones a little further from where they landed. As the first cushion flies, the heron jolts up into the air, with its prehistoric squawk, and heads for a tree at the far point in the cove. I hunch low in the back left corner of the stern, holding on, my fingers under the edges of the fiberglass deck at the sides where there is a gap left for rain and spray to escape to the bilge. The pike throws itself around the deck. The sides of the boat are too high for it to get back to the water. The oars follow, awkwardly rotating, blade over end over blade, once or twice until, gawky, their broad ends trip on the water and the oars angle down and pierce the water, then bob awkwardly as they sink.

I know I could make it to shore. No problem. But we are on the other side of the river, at least six miles down river from the pier. I would have to find a phone and explain to too many people why I was stranded.

A spare gas tank splashes in a bellyflop. The perch we caught. His deck chair. The Danish. His newspaper. I huddle in the corner until the only things left in the boat are me, the pike still slapping around the boat, my grandfather's rods and reels. His thermos. Him. With a silver slash of steel blade, his hunting knife severs the rope that holds us to the anchor, and he starts the boat up. His lines still out, their poles bend like willow limbs in a strong wind as he tears too fast out of the cove, revs the engine full, and throws the boat over waves and wakes back up the river to his mooring and home. I huddle, the day gone wild and frightening, bleak and unsure.

We surge straight and fast across the river, no mind paid to smaller boats, till we get to his buoy. He ties up, takes the pike into the skiff with him and putts back to the pier. He gets smaller as he goes and fades from color to silhouette. As he marches up the pier to his car, the pike swings from his stringer, still flapping and fighting. I watch his car disappear up the steep beach road going home. He never said a word. Nor did I. I have made myself as small as possible, crouching against the boat's ribs in the back left corner. Alone now, I listen as silence grows loud. No people are in the water or on the beach. No geese or swans honk and hiss in the shallows. Only crows break the silence, filling the hollow sky now and then, their grating metal caws announcing the presence of dead fish washed ashore.

My mother told me much later, when I finally felt able

to recount this series of events, that she knew something was wrong when my grandfather drove in fast and slammed the car door so hard that it might have broken the window. He had broken car windows before. She was afraid to go next door and ask what was wrong, what I had done, where I was. After a while, when I didn't follow him home, she drove down to the beach. I saw her car coming down the beach hill and ducked down, peering carefully through gaps in the bundle of tarp my grandfather had neglected to snap over the boat. She got out and walked out the pier to the skiff's slip, looked out at the boat. Finally, she walked back to the car, climbed in, drove away. I stayed in the boat as the sun moved from right above towards the west, letting my body bake on the gritty fiberglass deck, letting the sun sear my skin rather than seeking shade in the packed prow or swimming to shore. Occasionally I rose to peek over the edge of the boat at the shore up the hill towards home. Waiting for I don't know what — perhaps for the feeling that my chest and belly were collapsing, that I was caving into myself, to ebb. Perhaps just hanging on to the last peace I thought I'd ever know. The sun burned down and the boat rocked, drifting far enough every once in a while to pull hard at its chain and then give in to its mooring a hundred and fifty yards off shore. And finally, I lowered my body down into the tepid dog days' river, without the armor of mineral oil and vaseline to protect me from stinging nettles, and I began a slow crawl shoreward, the tentacles of nettles caressing my exposed flesh, burning, the ropy lengths of tall seaweed reaching almost to the surface and winding their strands around my legs and arms, pulling and dragging at me until I could only swim like a retriever, legs and arms spinning up close to the body, my chin pointed up and towards the beach. By the time I got to the shore, welts like red varicose veins were rising wherever the nettles' tentacles had caressed me.

2:11 A.M., September 17, 1973

My grandfather sleeps on his back *au naturale*. I pass the open door of the room he sleeps in, my parents' room, on my way to bed. In the light from the bathroom, left on so he doesn't wake up in confusion, I can see quite clearly that his balls are shrivelled like prunes, gnarled like the shells of black walnuts. But pale like anemic chicken livers. Maybe mauve. The door is open so I can hear him if he calls. Night after night for almost two weeks now, I've helped him sit up and then shouldered him down from my parents' tall post bed where he is sleeping during his visit. Guide and crutch, I half carry him to the toilet so he can urinate. I have gotten to know the contours of his big-boned old body, with its flaccid and pale flesh, long white whiskers sprouting from his chest like the wires of broken springs spiralling through a chair seat. He is six-four, but weak. He feels fragile to me — I worry as I guide and support that my fingers' pressure on his ribs might rub his crepe paper skin away and he might bleed.

In the middle of the night, I go to him when he cries out "Sis!" and wakes me. It interests me that he calls me this. Sis is the name he's always called Mom, which confused me when I was a kid. Mom was his *daugh*ter, not his sister. For no reason I can really recall, I eventually knew that for him his women were sort of generic. He called my sisters and my cousins Sis. He called mom Sis and my grandmother, his wife, Mom. I was four-teen before I realized that my grandmother and I shared the same first name. Elizabeth.

But now, at night, he calls out Sis and *I* go, to balance his near two hundred pounds of bone and flesh, stagger-stepping him from the bed through the dark bedroom to the brightly lit bathroom. I hold him up in front of the toilet, my arm around his waist as if in a hug, while he drapes his long skinny penis over the long warped fingers of his right hand and lets go a yellow stream in stops and starts, a trickle, a rush, a trickle.

It would be easier for us both, but he just will not sit down to pee. He is not shamed that I stand there, twenty, full-breasted and firm, supple and strong, lush, holding him while I brace myself against the cold tile wall so we won't fall. He says, "Girls sit." I wonder if he knows which Sis I am. I watch and wonder if he's unembarrassed because I'm just family.

During the day, he seems to know I'm a granddaughter, though he still calls me Sis. I keep him entertained, bake apple pies and let him eat them warm with butter and slabs of sharp yellow cheddar. Today, when I pressed the knife through the cheese, I remembered one night when I ate alone with my grand-parents at their house. Though they lived fifty yards from our back door, I hardly ever ate any meals at their table on my own. But this night, I think Mom was still in Annapolis in the hospital after having my new sister, Kathy, and that Dad was visiting. I was just seven.

My grandmother brought a hot apple pie to the table, sweet-scented steam rising gustily through the brown-edged A for Apple. As she went back to the kitchen to get the butter she always slipped in between the upper crust and the hot fruit before she passed a slice, Granddaddy winked at me and whispered, "Watch this, Bets." Then he called out, "Bring some cheese, Mom?"

My grandmother came back, anger stretching eyes to slits, her lips to lines, butter plate in her hand, and snapped that if he wanted to spoil her good pie with rat cheese to damn well get it himself. And he did. And then he began to eat his hot pie with thick slices of cheese, sassy lip-sucking and mm-mms with each full mouth. Grandmother steamed in silence. Granddaddy offered me a slice of cheese, and I almost took it, like a fish to bait. But it was bait, and nowadays I think he meant it as bait. It was too much of a test of my guts allegiance. I wanted, suddenly, to just leave, so my slice hardly touched, I said I was too full to eat *any*thing and could I be excused. And excused I went, out into the surprisingly warm mid-March evening, across the wide yard, and back to the safe upstairs of my home. Lifting the window facing down on their house, I watched and listened. Through their opened back door, I heard my grandmother's voice rise up and his roar answer.

2:17 A.M., September 18

I am keeping him entertained by playing the guitar and singing. "Waltzing Mathilda, waltzing Mathilda, will you come a waltzing Mathilda with me?" I sing that song at least fifteen times a day. It seems to be his favorite. He always has liked what Grandmother used to call "those bawdy songs" — those raucous, hip-slapping, stomping songs. He never liked sweet or bittersweet or just plain sad or bitter songs, and he had no use at all for classical music. Mostly, the songs he likes have some sex to them, but when I was a kid and he came into the house while I was practicing the piano, the best I could do was to stop wrestling with Clemente or Schubert and play something he liked. The "Little Brown Jug" or "Blue Tail Fly." Some polka. He liked the beat. Nowadays I do know a few truly bawdy songs I can sing to him, and a few I shouldn't, but today I sang those too. "Don't You Feel My Leg (Don't You Make Me High)" . . . "Woman Be Wise" . . . "Let Me Be Your Blender, Babe." They keep him happy, particularly the blender song when I get to whipping, chopping and pureeing. He slaps his thigh and laughs and calls me Sis. It helps us pass these days waiting for someone to come home so I can go back to school.

2:13 A.M., September 19

He was only here about thirty-two hours when he got to Mom so badly that she finally just threw some things in her car and drove off. I don't blame her. I should be worried, but right now I can't say I feel much. Dad is gone on business. I have always been one of those people who can smooth things out between people, but with Granddaddy here, I have met my match. I sent Kath off to stay with her friend, Lisa. My little sister has such a temper. She tolerates no seeming sin against her thirteen-year-old self. My grandfather has always been quick to zero in on sore spots, like a yellow jacket to a rotten spot on a windfall pear, and my sister has got a bunch of sore spots these days. She does not know this man like I do. She would not be careful. She has yet to learn caution.

So it's just him and me, this grandfather and me. If I have to be the one to take care of him with no adults around to help, because right now, even almost at twenty-one, I don't feel much like an adult in some ways, well, I certainly don't need my little sister acting out. I need to keep cool and tend to the immediate.

Today I added to my repertoire. "Alberta let your hair hang low. Alberta let your hair hang low. I'll give you more gold, than your pockets will hold, Alberta let your hair hang low" and I baked another pie and sliced up the cheddar. No problem. It's sort of getting routine now.

10:32 P.M., September 20

The smell of him is beginning to get to me. I can help him to the toilet at night so he makes it on time, but I am not sure how to get him clean of daily sweat and armpits. I have suggested a bath, but he doesn't want one. He asks, "What have I done to get dirty, Sis?" It's not that he's modest. He just does not want to get wet and chilled, and I can understand that, but still. There's a stand-up shower I might shove him into, but if his knees give way like they do at times, he'll fold up like some collapsible chair, and I'll have a hell of a time getting him out of that narrow space without hurting us both.

3:41 A.M., September 21

After eight days, I have cracked. I put a step stool in the bathroom this evening and when he called Sis and he finished his pee, I as gently as possible forced him to sit on the stool while I ran soapy hot water in the sink and sponged him down. He whined. Scary. "Aw Sis, don't. It's cold. I'm cold. It's cold. I'm cold." He was keening. I never knew what that sound really was till now. His voice rising like a high pitched siren, like the ones in war movies that keen over London when the Nazi bombers are zeroing in. "You're killing me Sis. You're killing me. Freezing me, Sis. Aw, Sis. Aw, Sis."

He scared me. He hit a high pitch and held it, long and clear, like the eerie howl of a beagle trailing a scent through a

cornfield in a raw and gray November dusk when the un-
cut stalks stand tall and dry and rustle, making sounds like
scratches on an old 78. Like the beagle whining on and on,
up one row, down the next, Granddaddy kept up his echoing
whine. A bath had seemed like a good idea. It was just water,
but he keened on and on with a terrible rhythm till he started
flailing, whipping the air with his arms like he was a windmill,
swatting at me like I was a gnat. I worked fast. I told him, "It's
warm water," trying to keep my voice sweet and get the soap
off him. When his bony forearm connected hard with my nose
and drew blood, I gave in.

I can't sleep. I keep hearing him telling me I'm killing him.

5:19 A.M., September 22

Around 4:00 this morning he tried to make the toilet on
his own and fell. He is so big, and one leg got bent under him.
He is so heavy. He wet himself and made a mess of my mother's
white rug. He's got a lump on his forehead and a bad bruise
coming up on his shoulder. I think he hit the bed when he fell.
I have been scared in my life, but this was different. I thought
he was dead, and it would have been my fault. I have promised
him no more baths and have been putting arnica and witch
hazel on the bruises. I can hear him breathing evenly now. I
feel so hollowed out.

12:15 P.M., September 22

So far, he's staying in bed today. Nice, though I feel guilty.
But I need a break from needing to do showtime all the time.
Time to think. The longer this goes on the more I remember.
I am a little unnerved by how much there is to remember, how
much I've forgotten.

I remember that when I was a kid, Granddaddy shot any cats that he saw come into the yard around his house. It didn't matter that they were the cats from the Schroederer's place down the road and that he knew it. He shot them anyway. Now Thomas P. Whiskers, big and black, our near feral tom, sleeps away his days on the foot of my parents' bed. Granddaddy seems tickled to have the company.

Grandmom didn't seem to care about the cats, but she was very protective of squirrels. She tamed them. Bunbuns. I still call them bunbuns, even though I try not to. She'd sit on the back steps humming out, "Here bunbun, come and get a peanut. Here bunbun here bunbun. Come and get a pea-nut." And those squirrels came. They took the nuts right out of her fingers without ever biting or scratching. Some would climb up her pants leg to get a nut. One old fat one with only half a tail would sit on her shoulder to get nuts. One day, my grandfather was outside by the steps. He had shorts on, no shirt, and I don't know why he was dumb enough to stand like he was, hips cocked, one leg slightly thrust forward, as he said something to my grandmother through the screen door. He stood there the way Grandmom stood when she called squirrels, and they really didn't need calling anymore. The fat one just came out of nowhere and scaled my grandfather's bare leg and chest right to his shoulder. I stood at the upstairs window facing their house and watched. I remember that I giggled once, as I watched, out of nervousness, I think.

11:22 P.M., September 22

Granddaddy has always been a tester and a judge, one of those people who has a place for everyone and always makes sure they know exactly where it is. I've learned that there are many people like that and that I am perversely drawn to them. Early conditioning, I suppose. I would have done anything to pass one of his tests with the very best grade. He used to lean towards me and smile and say, "Hey Bets. How are you?" and he'd squeeze my knee or elbow joint until I thought he'd press his fingers through and pinch my lower arm or leg right off. I'd smile into his brown eyes and say, "I'm fine. Just fine." But I wasn't and tears always oozed just enough from the corners of my eyes to give me away.

But to be fair, it wasn't just us kids he tested. Once he squeezed my father's right hand so hard in a handshake that my father brought his left fist up into Granddaddy's sternum and evicted the wind out of him. His eyes hardened to marbles, but his smile stayed in place.

4:44 A.M., September 23

I can't sleep. When I try I get trapped somewhere between sleep and waking. In the doze-zone. Paralysis. The house is so quiet. I am just sitting here in my bed listening for something. Keeping some vigil. And remembering. They say your life passes before your eyes as you drown. For days now I have found myself drowning in memories, wading through the now, then suddenly caught in a rip tide of the forgotten. Brains are attics with many trunks, often musty, a different key for each lock. And the trunk lids fly up and open without warning. Today, as I sat by his bed and played and talked, he started talking about the river, the fishing that was so much a rhythm of my life. He lay there recalling trips with my cousin Tim and Uncle Carver, with Mr. Peterson and Mr. MacCroirie. I was the one who went out with him most, yet it seems like he doesn't recall that. He said, "You were good at catching those minnows, Sis, and you were good at catching those eels."

"I was pretty good at other things too," I responded. "I caught my share of fish."

"Yeah," he snorted, "fishing up golf balls over near Sherwood Forest."

In my head, the lid of a trunk flung itself sharply open with the squawk of a startled great blue heron and the jolt of a boat moving too fast and direct across the wakes of other boats. I had, until this moment, forgotten that fish, that pike I caught, consumed a decade ago by Mr. MacCroirie and his wife, the neighbors to whom Granddaddy gave it along with a tall tale, a fish story of him struggling to bring it into the boat, with no net and too light a weight of line. I felt again the sun, the stillness of the moored boat, the grit of the deck, the fear of that day gone wild. At the edge of the woods beyond my parents' bedroom window, the crows of 1973 called back those crows on the shore ten years ago, and I felt again my own body caving into itself.

"Those were good days on that Severn River," he said, that frail old man lying comfortable in my parents' bed, pleased that a cat he would have shot ten years ago lay curled up at his feet. I sat very still, for a long while, and watched him and my black tom cat doze, knowing that all *his* river memories were sunlit.

How is it, I wonder, that we can forget our lives?

Baptism I
Vegetable Man

There was a vegetable man. An African American great-great-grandfather with large, strong teeth who, from mid-June into September, worked a regular route that took him down our lane once a week. No matter how many times my grandmother and mother shushed him, my grandfather would say "You can set your clock by that nigger." At that time, I could only respond to the lesser lie. The Vegetable Man usually came the same day of the week, but what time he actually arrived depended on his customers' needs and his own need for gossip, on whether he was alone or had a great grandchild along helping, on the weather, the state of the road, the degree of pain in his old mule's arthritic hips, and the extent to which the old man felt like pushing the endurance of his equally arthritic wagon, with its flat wooden roof and its baskets of vegetables. No one could set any clock by him. Perhaps the illusion that anyone could had something to do with how far away we could hear him before he finally turned into our road and came into sight. When he was moving, he sang out "Vegetable Man . . . Vegetable Man . . ." over and over, evenly, rhythmically. I know. I sang the words under my breath to myself during the summer days between his appearances.

His song, audible long before his cart was visible, stopped when he stopped for business or for talk. Sometimes those silences were long enough that they became eerie. I worried that he'd stopped for good and at the heart of the worry I felt that were he not to come, the day would be unable to move forward. The longer the silence, the more we'd all consciously keep our ears cocked, listening for him to pick up his song and cast it toward us. Sometimes my mother or grandmother would say, "Run see if you can hear that Vegetable Man," and I would hop on my bike and ride out the road, concentrating on hearing, and without fail I would eventually hear him or sight him in the distance. Then I would race back to report, "He's at MacComers'" or "He's at Welsh's" and "He's still on his way." Then we'd continue with our work or play as though we were not waiting, hearing his voice pick up its tune then stop, song and silence. Sometimes we could hear him coming for an hour. Sometimes it seemed we could hear him coming all morning long. The Vegetable Man's song did much more to whet our appetites than future songs we'd hear, the bells of Good Humor and the carnival refrain of Mr. Frostee.

The Vegetable Man's mule, Isaiah, had a sweet attitude and long ears, silky like a rabbit's, and Isaiah loved to have those ears fondled. Unaware of the irony, I'd always steal a carrot for Isaiah from our refrigerator or my grandmother's. The

Vegetable Man always had ripe corn and muskmelons and tomatoes a week or two before our own gardens got to producing the serious vegetables. The Vegetable Man also sold raspberries, blueberries, and gooseberries, crops my grandmother and parents had given up on because of the skill with which mockingbirds negotiated every protective barrier they dreamed up. The Vegetable Man played a mouth harp and told us kids dark, scary stories, mostly Biblical in origin but shifted just enough to make them more current, very regional, and very secular. And when the Vegetable Man had help in the form of someone to urge Isaiah along, he made, right before our eyes, the small blown glass ships and swans and castles and cows and pigs and roosters that always nestled in amongst the more gentle vegetables. He blew them right before our eyes.

To my mind, the Vegetable Man was a major event in the routine of summer. To my grandmother's mind, the Vegetable Man served a purpose but dished out gratuitous frivolity, particularly when it came to his gossip and blown glass dust-catchers. Of the gossip, my grandmother feigned disinterest, usually chiding him for having his nose where it had no business, but she partook and contributed and passed what she heard along to Mrs. MacCrorie and Mrs. MacCrorie to Mr. Gold and Mr. Gold to Mrs. Schriner. Of his vegetables, my grandmother was a critical buyer, loudly ripping the husks back from ears of corn, thumping melons and squeezing tomatoes until the Vegetable Man would intercede on their behalf. "You do them justice, Ma'am, yes you do," he would carefully but obliquely plead as his hands followed the disordering path hers made through his baskets. He'd lightly resettle peppers and tenderly pull husks back up the length of ears to cover their naked kernels. Sometimes he would be more direct, saying something like, "They give you nothing but good eating and you assault them so Ma'am." He would defend them, always with a smile. Usually my grandmother would cease her fretting with his fruits and buy the very ears she'd partially stripped and then discarded. Other times, she would keep right on prodding and poking while she grilled him as to where these vegetables had come from. He claimed he grew them at home with the help of his family. She made clear that perhaps she suspected that he stocked up at the Lexington Market in downtown Baltimore. "Those people can't be trusted" she would say, but announcing that she suspected him of buying his vegetables was a matter of saving face. He grew his own. I had seen his extended family's yards and yards of gardens when my parents drove by his house going somewhere, recognizing him as he sat on his porch. Isaiah stood slouching, head hanging, asleep in a small paddock by a small sloping lean-to. I figured that my grandmother had seen his gardens as well and just pretended not to have seen them, for if she admitted that he actually grew the vegetables himself, then she admitted that he annually beat her in her highly competitive race to be the first to have ripe tomatoes, corn, and melons from her own garden.

But it never failed that every day he stopped at our houses, he and my grandmother would debate his honor. If he had bought the vegetables at the Lexington Market in Baltimore, he would postulate, he would have needed a pick-up to get to the market because he lived nearly forty miles outside the city; and if he had a truck, he would postulate further, why would he be driving an old worn-down mule toward its grave instead of driving that pick-up he would have to have to get to the Lexington Market? In return, my grandmother would speculate that the mule and the wagon had more beguiling sales appeal than a pick-up would, and that no one would hear him singing out his vegetables over the engine of a pick-up, to which he would counter, "Why wouldn't I just blow that pick-up's horn, Ma'am?" Back and forth they'd go, bickering, bickering about where his vegetables came from, dickering about how much he charged as opposed to how much she would pay. Eventually, when Isaiah the mule reached his grave, the Vegetable Man did begin making his rounds in a pick-up, aged, black and rusted. He did not blow its horn, though, if indeed the horn worked, and its engine gave no challenge to his call. But neither Isaiah the mule nor that pick-up could have ever gotten him into Baltimore and back in fewer than days. I don't know how many, but it would have been days.

My grandmother would sometimes speculate to him that he had a driver, a son or the like, maybe even hired one with all the money he made charging so much for his vegetables. "Those people can't be trusted," she would say to whoever listened, but only after the Vegetable Man had gone off. I am sure if he'd heard her say that, he might have stopped calling out to us.

One summer for some weeks he had with him a teenaged grandson, John Ellison, and a great granddaughter, Rebekka Rochelle. John Ellison, probably fourteen, dark and brooding, made no eye contact no matter how many times my grandmother, or one of the other older women who met the wagon where we did, would ask him what cat had got his tongue. Rebekka Rochelle was about my age, ten, and like most of the African American kids my age, wore her hair in corn rows and braids. My grandmother called the preadolescent kids like Rebekka Rochelle *pickaninnies.* The word *pickaninnies* sounded magical to me — elves, fairies, poetry — but the way she said it felt wrong. I look the word up now and find it designated, in italics, *Offensive.* I look at its origins, *pickin* (West African) or *pickney* (Jamaican) meaning — as does the Spanish word *pequeno* — *little, small, a small child.* Magic and elfin the word may have sounded then, but it is one come into American English through Creole and slavery. Its offensiveness has been titrated into it over time through people and their choices in usage.

To be honest, I wanted corn rows myself, a desire my grandmother made short shrift of. When rows became fashionable for anyone, I was one of the first in my circle to try them. My hair was too flyaway.

One of my unspoken wishes was to ride with the Vegetable Man, particularly on the days when Rebekka Rochelle rode along and John Ellison drove and called out the vegetables. Rebekka Rochelle rode beside him when she was not minding the vegetables, and the Vegetable Man blew glass in the section he cleared in the back of the wagon. The apparatus seemed simple — a wooden box, protected on top with a sheet of metal to which had been secured a simple Bunsen burner. How the flame was fueled I am not sure. But with a variety of blowing instruments, some for the mouth, and one that was a pedalled bellows like on my Aunt Edith's air driven organ, he would ignore the goings-on of the vegetables and make figures and ornaments. Some were just for hanging, others just for sitting. All began with clear glass tubes and the Vegetable Man gave the impression that he never knew what delicate item would emerge, as though the glass tubes came with their own exquisite secrets.

John Ellison did not seem impressed, but then with John Ellison it would have been hard to tell. Rebekka Rochelle was impressed, but she also took her grandfather's glass blowing for granted. I imagined her bedroom airy and sunlit and graced by rainbows from ornaments hanging from every window, sitting on every surface, creating dancing flickering spectrums on white walls. When I asked her about the room I imagined for her, she looked at me, crossed her eyes, and said, "You forget I've got seven sisters older than me. There's no one room for one." Later when she thought to ask me if I had my own room, I thought of all the china horses I stabled there and lied, said I had to share too, of course.

The Vegetable Man sold the pieces of his craft, a dollar for small ones, three dollars for medium and five for large. In a box in my attic I have two small ones, a ship and a swan, carefully wrapped in tissue. I bought the first by accident. Rebekka Rochelle offered to let me look at one she was playing with and it slipped through my fingers to the road. She just shrugged, and the Vegetable Man said it was of no consequence, but my grandmother sent me to my pig bank for a dollar to pay for what I'd broken, a transaction I was glad to make. But when I passed two Franklin fifty-cent pieces to Rebekka Rochelle, she snuck me a ship, hissing, "Just don't drop it. Look like nothing. Just put it in your pocket, girl." So I did. No one noticed. The second is a swan my mother bought for me later that summer. I think she liked them too, even if they did catch dust.

Decapitating Crocuses on Easter Morning

It is early on Easter Sunday, hours before church, way before time to go and see what the Easter Bunny has left. I know the basket will be exquisite. But I will not sneak downstairs to see it. Last night, after my younger sister went to bed, my mother and I gently pressed green straw and pink angel hair into two baskets, one for me, even though I know, at nine, that the Easter Bunny is my father and mother, and one for my little sister who, at two, knows the Easter Bunny is *real*. Such a believer, she will not even recognize the eggs she and I carefully colored yesterday afternoon. Into pungent vinegar water we put — no, I let *her* put — the hard, mysterious pellets from which dye explodes into minute tornadoes streaming in all directions, coloring the water. These pellets are my second favorite part of Easter. My favorite part is the egg hunt after church. I am good at finding things. I know, too, that this will be my last egg hunt. I am too fast, too good, and though I can let my sister discover the joy of the coloring pellets, I cannot be so generous under pressure in a horde of kids when it comes to the competitive hunting of colored eggs. What, after all, would be the point?

As my mother and I began the baskets, my other sister, who at sixteen has declared herself too old for a basket, carefully painted our colored eggs — adding little flowers and birds and clouds and bunnies and crosses surrounded by daffodils. Her arched artist's hand gracefully tapped animate, delicate moments onto otherwise plain, sometimes dull Easter eggs. My best creative coloring efforts are half and halfs — yellow around one half, small end to middle, purple around the other, big end to middle. Usually an uneven belt of gray sludges a circle mid-egg where I just can never keep the colors from touching. My worst creative efforts are attempts to create new colors out of two or three colors, resulting always in dull brown. With impatience at my annual ignorant abuse of color, my sister has painted a peach flower with emerald leaves, shiny and raised as if enameled, on the brown egg, asking me why I want to color a special white egg, the kind we only get at Easter, so it looks like the brown eggs we eat every day.

"It was an accident," I confess, defensive.

"You do not understand color," she announces, a judgment of my perception, a judgment she will repeat over the years to come. And she is right. I do not understand how colors in paint respond to each other, how thick or thin pigments meld to other hues. I understand how the prisms of chandelier crystals paint rainbows on the dining room wall and how outboard motors cast circular oil rainbows on water, but that does not help me in the daily use of color.

My sister takes my ugly egg and makes it beautiful. I can tell from the way she hisses air out her narrow nostrils that she is impatient with me, that she makes the egg beautiful to make a point. I know that next Easter there will probably be another such egg, and that does not bother me too much. Mostly, I am content to envy her artist's hand. I love to watch her work with such care, whether on an egg, a canvas, a wall mural, or the wooden canoe she paints each year with Native American designs. I love to watch pictures and shapes emerge from nothing. I lean as close as she'll let me and breathe carefully, so I am quiet and so my breaths do not tickle the hairs on her arm. When she has painted all she cares to, we carefully balance the eggs on their carton to dry.

I go up to my bed in the small room I have recently moved into on the second floor of our small Cape Cod. The stairs to the second floor rise up from a square connecting hall between the back and front of our little house. There is a shutter door between this hall and the dining room that I pull closed behind me after saying good night. It is shut every night, but it is only taboo for us kids to pass through it on special mornings, like Easter and Christmas. We wait to be invited into those mornings, and that is okay. The graceful, overstuffed baskets of spring pastels and dark chocolates, the beauty of the Christmas tree first seen in pre-dawn, its lights the only lights in the world — those are worth waiting for an invitation to see.

At the top of the stairs, I climb up for a moment on the old flat-topped, attic trunk beneath the double window that gazes over the side lawn to my grandparents' house. Although their dinner has been over for hours, their kitchen light is on. I can see my grandmother at the sink. This Easter falls on my grandmother's birthday. I wonder if she is washing up after making herself a cake. Spice. Caramel glaze. Raisins.

I often watch from this trunk, noting the movements of

adults gardening, hanging wash, the silent movement of their lips as they converse. They pull in and out of the driveways, crunching gravel under their tires, and I can tell by the way they move, by the way they leave their cars, by their faces' ease or rigidity, if they are pleased or displeased. When I watch the adults from this window, I feel a distance larger than the space of air and lawn between us. I am sometimes embarrassed when I am amongst them, not because I have seen them do anything I should not have, but because I am conscious of my watching, conscious of this stranger in me who observes silently, who takes mental notes of their actions.

I climb off the trunk and head away from the window, running my finger lightly along the raw pine two-by-four railing, sticky in spots with resin and rough with splinters, protecting my sister and me from walking out into space over the stairs in the dark. My room, small and blue, is straight ahead in the back right corner of our house. My sister's larger room takes up the front half of the second floor. After I have crawled between covers and am reading, she, too, comes up to bed, tells me to turn out my light, and secludes herself in her room with a click of her door's iron lever latch. I hear her move around. I do not know what she does in there behind that closed door. At times I try to spy, but she almost always catches me.

When my little sister moved out of her crib into my bed downstairs and I was moved upstairs, my parents let me use a large closet at one end of my big sister's room. It is my office. There is a single wide shelf I use as a desk. There is a trunk against the wall opposite the shelf that I use as a cot or a sofa or a jail cell, depending on who I am and what world I am inhabiting. On the pressed-cardboard wall above the desk, I have pinned my names, a black paper horse with Alec Ramsey in white crayon, a stolen queen of hearts with Bret Maverick's signature, a cardboard sheriff's star that says Marshall Earp, a plastic magnifying glass glued to a cardboard name plate — Nancy Drew. On the desk surface, I neatly line up pens and stack half-used, yellow legal pads I have borrowed from my father's desk. Recently, I acquired a half-used pad of graph paper, pale green with lines making small squares. My mother and grandmother use such paper to create designs for needle-point and dresses, my grandfather and father for planning out woodwork. My older sister uses it to imagine dimensions for her paintings. The paper excites my imagination and seems ultimately more useful than other paper. Maybe I will use it to chart a diagram of the river and mark the best places for catching crabs and different fish. Maybe I will use it to make a secret map of secret places.

I try to be in this closet when my sister is in her room, but whether she will let me is under serious negotiation. The closet is mine, but I cannot use it when she is there unless she allows me to walk the narrow public path she has demarcated with invisible lines drawn by the sweeping of her arms between the door of the closet and the door of the room. She worries about my passing through when she is away and thinks these lines will keep me from snooping around her painting table and her bureau, just as invisible lines have always kept me on my side of the back seat of our orange and black Ford station wagon. She is right. I look, even stop for long moments and peruse her surfaces carefully, but I for now touch nothing. I tread my narrow right-of-way carefully. She would know if I stepped out. And I never dare go into the part of her room to the left of the door where no public path exists. I know she would know if I did.

My big sister stays up late, her radio singing . . . "she wore bluuuue velvet . . . in 1816, I took a little trip . . . it was a one-eyed, one-horned, flying purple people eater . . . *who* wears short shorts?" These lyrics reach me under my covers where I, with flashlight, embrace *The Black Stallion's Revenge*. My door stands open. I am afraid to be closed in and rue that fear. Eventually, my sister passes my doorway going to the half-bath we share and says, oh so casually, "I'm telling Mama." Flashlight out, I soon fall asleep, only to wake early, just before dawn, like I do on Christmas and birthdays, on the days of swim meets and annual class trips to the Smithsonian or the Baltimore Zoo.

As the light begins to gray the sky, I slip out of bed and go to the top of the stairs and listen. Sleep silence. The bird in the dining room mutters quietly under its white night sheet. From my parents' bed just to the right down the stairs, my father's wuffling snore murmurs like a wheezing of early spring breeze. I want to go down and peek but dare not. Doing so would ruin the surprise, and that, like Christmas, is what Easter is all about. Surprise by beauty and color, by the familiar made special.

Besides, I know what will be there. At my and my little sister's places at the table, there will be the baskets of green and pink grass nestling the wonderful colored eggs. There will be amazing Easter candy eggs — the size of jelly beans but universes apart. All colors, some swirled — blue and white, purple and white, gold and white — like precious stones. Some will be white and coconut, some layers, egg within egg, strawberry within vanilla. There will be chocolate eggs in green and yellow foil, a hard sugar egg with a vista inside, and a chocolate buttercream fruit egg the size of a large goose egg. I will get thin slices of that for dessert at night for weeks to come. All told, the basket will last me to the fourth of July parade in

Catonsville and the Fireman's Fair on the Governor Ritchie Highway. I will take the plain, hard-boiled eggs without painted pictures to school in lunches with carefully folded wax papers of salt. The painted eggs and the vista egg will eventually join their predecessors who have gone unbroken from earlier Easters and are in my underwear drawer.

So, I wait. I kill time. I am so quiet that I can hear the air whistle at my ears. I creep back to my room, get my book and flashlight, for it is only dawn, and tiptoe noiselessly back to the head of the stairs. I set the book on the trunk under the window. I do not read. Instead, I listen. I move carefully on a path back and forth, stairs to room to stairs, with my much-practiced Indian stealth. It is a powerful feeling to be the only one awake, the one who will first smell the acid smoke of a fire or hear the robber slitting the kitchen window screen with a sharp knife. I am a good waiter, although when I wait, I can do little else. The act of waiting, itself, absorbs me. I move and pause. I listen. I stalk the first sound of someone waking downstairs; and even then, when I catch that first sound, I'll wait on the middle of the stairs like a statue until I am discovered and invited down to the opening of the shutter doors into the dining room and Easter.

In one silent circling of the upstairs hall, I go over to the double window at the top of the stairs, climb up on the old wooden attic trunk there, and look out, down across our side yard over to where my grandparents' meets ours. There is a wire fence with a wooden picket gate separating their yard from ours. The hood ornaments on my grandparents' cars glint silver. In the early light of dawn, gray with just a touch of icy yellow, I see a shadow move. After a moment, I recognize that the shadow is my grandmother, on her knees under the

Bartlett pear, in weeding position, working the ground. It is not unusual for her to be up in the pre-dawn, and that she has been weeding for a while is clear from the small mound near the edge of the circular bed. But there's something more. In that flower bed around the trunk of that tree, white and purple and yellow crocus blossoms lie on the dark soil rather than dancing above it; and as I watch, I realize that she is snipping more blossoms off as she moves slowly round the tree. One by one, blossoms topple to the dirt to rest beside their stems. Her silver scissors flash, the brightest light yet in the dawn, as they sacrifice the earliest of spring flowers on Easter morning. Like the heads rolled by guillotine blades in a book about the French Revolution I found just the week before. Nothing can be done. No vase can save these crocuses.

I hate what I am seeing, but I cannot tear my eyes away. In my stomach, a lump swells. Methodically, her scissors flash silver. They are her sewing shears. "The sewing shears are not allowed outside. And they cut nothing but cloth." I have heard her say that so many times. As I watch, I get this feeling I have come to know well. I am teased about it if someone realizes I am feeling it. I even try to tease myself. I try to now. It is my "nobody loves me, everybody hates me sitting in the garden eating worms" feeling, my "just a little petunia in an onion patch" feeling. It is the feeling of having suddenly swollen up and hollowed out, filled with emptiness, filled with nothing. It is the feeling too of tears rising in a stinging and hot flood behind my eyes. I chant at me as I kneel there on the trunk watching. "Just a little petunia in an onion patch, onion patch, onion patch, just a little petunia in an onion patch, crying the live-long day." These taunts don't work. I tell myself I have done nothing wrong, but the emptiness now fills my whole diaphragm. And though I feel as though there is not a thing inside me, I feel too that I could burst.

And I watch, paralyzed, until my grandmother rises and dusts her hands off slowly against each other. I can almost feel the cool, raspy dirt against palms, smell its earthiness. I can tell by her rigid, spare shoulders that she is angry. As if feeling me watching, she looks up at the window and I duck, fast, back off the trunk, step back again, and back soundlessly, carefully until I am in my room and then in my bed where I curl on my left side and face the blue wall. Eventually, my sister rises and, after washing her face, goes downstairs, leaving the prickly scent of Noxzema in the air. Eventually, my father comes up the stairs and calls into my room from the doorway, sing-songy, "Someone's playing opossum." I want to yell out that I am *not* playing opossum. But I don't. I just lie there, eyes lightly closed, very still, until my father goes away. His voice is soon replaced by my mother's cool palm on my forehead. So cool and soft, I could almost doze for real, but I rise, feigning awakening. They ask how I feel. I am fine, I say, just fine.

Downstairs, my older sister sits reading at the table in front of her chocolate fruit and nut egg the size of the elephant bird egg they have at the Smithsonian. My little sister has her candy out of the basket and is making little piles of like kinds — red jelly beans, white coconut eggs, yellow jelly beans, jewelled swirls. In our kitchen, which faces my grandparents' kitchen, I hear the contented murmur of my parents' voices as they concoct a Sunday breakfast. I hear the whir of the blender as it first blends frozen orange concentrate with water and then whips eggs for an omelet. Sausages spit fragrant grease in the iron skillet on the stove. As I pass through the dining room, I ignore the table where my basket sits, a yellow ribbon bowed at the crest of its wicker handle, and go to the back door and look out across the yards to the pear tree, its buds showing pink-white tips of flowers pressing out against their green lapels. I know the crocuses' heads lie wilting and dying beneath the tree, neatly separated spikes of stem and flowers making a grue-some parody of Easter eggs ready for the hunt, just out of sight. I know they are there. I want my mother to know too.

So I ask, "What is wrong with Grandmommy's crocuses?" as though I can really see the decapitated flowerheads over or through the hedge that grows from the fence between our back yards out to the narrow road at the end of our drives.

"'Crocus' is the plural form," my mother intones, then asks, "What do you mean?"

I have overestimated. She is taller and can see out the win-dow over the counter where she stands, but she cannot see the ground at the base of the pear either. Either she does not note my error or else she lets it pass. "What do you mean?" she repeats.

"The crocus," I start. "Something is wrong with Grand-mommy's crocus." I pause. "They look all broken off." I add, "From the window upstairs."

My mother says "Oh dear" and comes to the door where I stand. She still cannot see what I know.

"Under the pear tree," I add. She goes out the door and follows the walk between the roses and boxwoods to the gate to Grandmother's house, glancing back my way when she sees the severed heads. My father continues his part in preparing breakfast. Before him on the counter mounds of omelet fil-ling grow. grated yellow cheese, minced onion and green pep-per, mushrooms, sliced hot dog. My mother stands at the gate, looking toward the base of the pear tree for a long moment, then comes back.

"Go sit down and get ready for breakfast," she tells me, then goes back out the door and toward her mother's house.

In the bright dining room, the brilliant morning rays paint crisp shadows of blinds and silhouettes of plants on the light green walls over the sideboard where silver servers and ladles and cut glass celebrate the sun. My little sister's basket is packed again and out of her reach. My father comes in and sits at the table to read us Sunday comics. *Mark Trail. Nancy. Peanuts. Li'l Abner.* The back door opens, shuts, and at my mother's call, he hands the comics to me and goes out to the kitchen. I continue where he left off. My younger sister, not content with my reading, begins to howl until I lift her from her chair and set her on the floor. She follows after our father. Over my parents' murmurs, the engine of my Grandfather's Buick roars to life and backs out of the drive with a spray of white gravel. His car zips past our house with only one possible destination. His boat. The river.

Next to my place at the table sits my basket. I pull it over and set my nostrils on its rough rim and feel the green straw tickle as I smell the sugary sweetness of chocolate and coconut within. After a bit, I reach in.

"Don't spoil your breakfast," my sister warns from behind her book.

I pull out the vista egg. Its sparkling, white surface, crusty with small hexagons of sugar, is bisected round the middle and from end-to-end by a ridge of green sugar garland knobbed with pink and yellow flowers. One end has been cut across and covered with clear, thin glass. Inside the egg is a miniature garden, white fence, grass and flowers, a rabbit, a duck, a deer, a blue sky, and a puff of white cloud.

My parents come in with plates of omelet and toast and

sausage. Breakfast starts. Breakfast ends. My big sister is singing a solo at church and goes upstairs to "put on her face," a new phrase she has begun to use regularly. It intrigues me as much as it distresses my mother. My father takes my little sister to get into her new Easter dress. As I move to join the exodus, hands on my shoulders stop me, turn me around, and my mother's eyes probe mine. "Do you know what happened to the crocus?" she asks.

"No," I answer. I could tell what I saw, but in the bright Easter morning I feel it unbelievable. I could tell what I saw, but I do not know anything. "No," I say, "No. I don't know what happened to the crocus." My mother turns and leaves me, saying to dress for church while she returns to my grandparents' house to see if her mother will be riding with us to Easter Service. For a moment, I return to my place at the table and sit a minute longer, studying the inside of the egg, imagining myself small enough to enter in.

Baptism II
My Grandmother
and the Colonel

Far back in the yard behind my house in a grove of maples and pussy willows, a spot cool even during the hottest July day, there is a shrub. That's what we call it, as if with a capital *S*: a Shrub. Its burgundy flowers are shaped like the East Indian brass bell that sits in the china closet — narrow stiff petals spaced evenly like the bell's claw around a central ball like the bell's clapper. The shrub scents hot humid evenings with hints of cloves and rose petals, whispers of cinnamon and allspice — mysterious and rich, sharp yet peaceful. The shrub itself stands eight feet tall and spreads eight feet wide. From the side that looks away from the house, there is an entrance into its core, a fragrant tent of dense foliage. I hide beneath it, sitting Indian style or lying flat out on the cool dirt. It provides clear vantage into my grandparents' back yard as well as my own and that of the neighbors behind us. At times, I slip in and out of sight simply to watch. At others, the shrub offers me retreat when life gets tense and I feel the need to disappear. It is evening, now, and dinner is over and life is tense. I have come to suspect, the last two weeks of this sultry July, that I may know something I should probably tell somebody. I am pretty sure I know what I know, but I don't know who I could tell or exactly why I would, even. I think my grandmother and the Colonel are in love, and I don't know what to do, how to do, if to do. And part of me thinks it's none of my business, except it is my business because I think they use me as their cover. Their routine begins like this.

First it's the asparagus in the early summer. My father and I cut our own, slipping the sharp blades of our knives into the soil around the stem and slicing the stalk just out of sight. We have located seven spots where the asparagus have replanted themselves, some spots quite far from the large garden in the back corner of our yard. My favorite plot is that of the asparagus which slipped out to the front yard and hide in the barberry hedge between our drive and my grandparents'. It's a trick to get them without getting sliced myself by the barberry thorns. My grandmother grows no asparagus, but the Colonel does.

His house is one of the two original houses on the peninsula, a stately huge white house, the front of which faces the river and looks off across to Sherwood Forest. His garden covers at least an acre, his orchard another. Several more acres of green lawn with tall ancient trees surround the house and its carriage house. By his garden is a tool shed as large as some of the new houses on the Ritchie Highway going into Glen Burnie. On one side, it has a door the size and height of a large dog door, which we kids use with discretion, when this or that haunt loses its charm. Once a short-term playmate, Axel, dropped a large rock from the shed's roof as I was crawling out the door. The rock landed on my left hand. Axel had hoped for my head and said as much. I was simply glad he missed and went for years before coming to realize that had the rock landed on my head as intended I might have died. Instead, my hand bore testimony to Axel's perhaps innocent attempt at murder. The back of the hand and each finger turned a lustrous purple, then yellow; each nail turned ebony and eventually fell off.

The early summer begins the annual encounters between my grandmother and the Colonel. He brings her bouquets of asparagus which she steams and eats with butter and black pepper and toast. My grandfather hates asparagus. My grandmother eats them lustily, as if nothing else on earth could taste as good.

The asparagus transform into yellow squash with straight necks, not crooked necked like we grow. The Colonel brings them in an oval woven basket which hangs from his arm like a cradle. Sometimes, nestled amongst the yellow squash are tiny zucchinis, *courgette*, the Colonel calls them. My grandfather calls them unripe yellow squash. My grandmother nibbles them raw. The Colonel brings her baby carrots he thins from his rows, the roots like silk, the greens still tiny ferns. Fennel bulbs and French breakfast radishes. The first pinches of basil. The Colonel grows herbs that then seem exotic, many sages, different thymes, rosemary pungent and piney. We grow traditional parsley. He grows Italian, Chinese, and mossy. He brings so much that this summer I ask him if he saves some for home. He chuckles, really chuckles, a confection of sound like heavy wooden dice rumbling in cupped hands. "There's plenty to go around," he says. "Just me and the missus" who is not too keen on vegetables, I induce. Not like Bess, my grandmother, who shares his love for things grown and green.

When it comes time for okra, which my grandmother boils and serves in a cream sauce, I pray not to have to sit down to dinner at her house. The white cream and the okra's natural thickening juices merge into a slime that makes spooning a small portion out of the bowl impossible. With the spoon I pick up the entire mass; then the bowl is taken from my hands and a generous portion is cut away from the whole of the mass and set on my plate where it oozes thickly up against the things I *like* to eat.

By okra time, my grandmother and the Colonel have progressed from polite offer and acceptance through catching up with family, through analysis of the changes on the peninsula and in Severna Park since the autumn before, to discussion of world events and the stock market. Unlike my grandfather, the Colonel enjoys talk with my grandmother about serious things, and I get to listen, which is something I do very well most of the time. They take me with them hunting wild vegetables and fruits. We cut tender poke like asparagus. Later we search for dewberries and canvass our well-known swamps for blackberries.

To hunt blackberries, one must dress right. There are chiggers and ticks, so we dust our lower legs and arms with yellow sulfur powder and tuck long pants into socks. The irony of this is lost on me. I hang out in these same woods and swamps daily in shorts and no shoes, but I never question the careful dress and sulfur when I go with my grandmother and the Colonel to pick berries. We carry aluminum buckets with wooden handholds at the crest of the handles. We load my wagon with berry boxes and I pull it as I follow them to where the road ends and a path dips down through Round Bay Woods toward Round Bay Swamp. The stands of berries there are the best, with canes easily arching twelve feet into the air, canes over an inch in diameter. The Colonel carries a machete, saying he will "carve a path through the vicious barbigerous jungle for us, ladies." I like the way the Colonel talks and I try to match him. "You will carve a path through barbigerous brambles," I counter.

"Oh that's good, dear, very good," he says, smiling at my grandmother.

Once when we are picking, a storm sounds in the distance. To my grandmother, the Colonel says, "Ah Bess, I sense *une coup de foudre*. We should start back to our respective homes. Come Betsy. We must not shilly-shally." *Coup de foudre coup de foudre coup de foudre* I mutter to myself all the way home. I have taken French after school since second grade. I know *coup* and I know *de*, but *foudre* is new. Once home I sneak into my sister's room and look it up in her *New Cassell's French Dictionary. Foudre* means a lot. Lightning, thunder, a thunderbolt. A sudden blow or calamity. Divine anger. Fulminations. Ah, love at first sight. A sudden intense bolt of love. *He sensed une coup de foudre.*

When the Colonel, my grandmother and I pick berries, which we do almost every day for two weeks each July, they give me the largest aluminum bucket because I am "so young and fast and such a good picker" and the Colonel cuts me a *cul de sac* into the deep center of the stand. The berries are glorious, immense black jewels ready to drop from their briary origins. He leaves me there, saying beware of cottonmouths, for they "love tender ankles as much as we love berries." I promise him that they'll just smell sulfur and think I'm another cottonmouth, and he leaves me. Quickly I lunge into plucking. First I am erratic for the best berry is everywhere I look. Eventually I calm and become mesmerized by the rhythm of picking, coming out of my reverie only when my pail needs to be emptied or the berries get too high for me.

Pick pick pick. Can can can. Jar jar jar. That's a central theme of every summer. Pies, flummery, jelly, and jam. Jars of peaches and pickles. Bags of sweet cherries for the freezer. Pick pick pick. I *love* it. Particularly the picking of what grows wild. I am the perfect hunter. I am the expert gatherer. I am agile and small. I climb trees with the skill of a spider monkey. I burrow through briars like Br'er Rabbit. And I have noticed this summer that I can pick more of anything by myself than my grandmother and the Colonel can together. I have noticed too that somehow, whatever we are picking, they always manage to keep apart from me, often staying out of my sight completely and for long periods of time — around a bend, behind the tall stand of blackberry canes. And they send me on errands they could just as easily do themselves. "Check the tide, Miss Betsy" or "Empty my pail, Miss Betsy." What is she going to do without a pail while I stop *my* picking to empty her pail? It's not that I mind doing errands. It's that I mind being sent off, letting them get out of my sight. But I am conscious, suddenly, of both the errands and the distance they put between themselves and me. The errands feel contrived, a way for my grandmother to check up on *me*. But perhaps I am making something of nothing.

This morning as I come out of my picking daze, I hear them ghostly on the outside of the blackberry patch. I hear the Colonel prefix or suffix just about every statement with "Bess, dear." I try to remember if he has always done that, but I can't recall for sure. Actually, I think not. But then, maybe so. When they are quiet, I have the same urge I do with my older sister when she is with a boy. I want to sneak up and see if they are kissing. Not that I expect them to really be kissing, but I will never know. One does not sneak up on a grandmother, however. *That* is a lesson I have learned several times and do not need to learn again. So I stop and try to listen hard, but I get distracted by my thoughts.

He's got a wife at home. To me, she's boring and stiff and always wears crisp dresses with small prints, collars, long sleeves with cuffs, and a narrow leather belt around her tiny tiny waist. My grandmother has to be held down by my aunt and mother to get a bra on her. Not that she's indecent. She just doesn't wear bras and my Aunt Edith is mortally shamed when we go someplace formal and my grandmother goes braless in her sharp gray wool skirt with its matching jacket, over a hand-crafted white blouse with tucked tucks and pleats running vertically and parallel on either side of the length of pearl buttons. My aunt swears she can see the shadow of my grand-mother's brown areola and nipples. She says it's indecent. My grandmother is anything but indecent. Even in a halter top, a design I think she created as a young farm wife for hot days of mowing and weeding, even in a halter top, her breasts don't show. But my aunt thinks otherwise, and next to the Colonel's wife my grandmother does seem somewhat undomesticated.

I follow behind them, now, as we head to our respective homes. I pull the wagon full of packed berry boxes, most of which will go home with me to my mother's kitchen. The Colonel and my grandmother walk ahead of me, mindless of me, talking and laughing. Her laugh rings strange in my ears. Lighter? More true? Am I wrong? Has she always laughed like that? The Colonel holds my grandmother's elbow as they walk. Has he always done that? When they talk, the one listening cocks his or her head toward the one speaking. Have they always done that? I can't recall. It's just now, this summer, my eleventh summer, that I think I am catching on to something I should have noticed before. I lag behind them, wondering if I were to stop would they even notice. I feel alone, as though they have entered some world that I am absent from. My older sister does that and would not notice if it were her and some boyfriend walking in front of me. So I stop. They continue on a few paces. Then my grandmother calls back, without even looking, "Come on, Miss Betsy. You are going to make dinner late."

Death
by African Violet

Syracuse University, 1972 We're *so* cool. My roommate and I hang out on our narrow dorm cots with their East Indian bedspreads. Sandalwood incense burns. We are speaking wisdoms when they strike us as we drink Tyrolia Pineapple Wine and smoke Newports. We are talking about who we have become, at least for the time. We have just recently learned to smoke. Not easy, but we persevered and we succeeded. We have also learned to drink Black Russians and shots of tequila straight, after licking Morton's salt off the back of our left hands, with no choking squinting grunting before we get to plunge the saving slice of lemon in between our front teeth and bite down hard. That biting of lemon reminds us of the women we see in late night old movies, fuzzy on our black and white, biting their own hands to silence the agonies of childbirth lest they and all with them be murdered by Union soldiers or Pawnees, lest they be shamed by older women who have been there and who look down from their years to deny younger women the truths of their experiences.

We know such older women already. Two live down the hall, our Resident Advisors, and they have denied us our homesickness and our problems with learning chemistry in an auditorium of five hundred. The thirty of us freshmen, except for weeping SueAnn, who has become Mormon and is transferring to Brigham Young next year, began avoiding the RAs week three. Now they prowl the halls, sniffing at doors for *eau de maryjane*, listening for male baritones after one in the morning, keeping note of all our vices as best they can. We wonder who they report to, who advises them. We contemplate them as we lie there puffing rings and trying to enjoy the sharp slice of menthol against the backs of our throats. My roommate wonders why they have pushed their cots together. I wonder how they will ever get through college if they keep trying to catch 30 people doing things they shouldn't, which we all do, all the time and with great variety. I mean, what are they going to *do* if they catch us? But we figure if the RAs haven't caught us feeding the four 100 percent male bluegrass band members that our hall of women tends like favorite pets in the empty room directly across the hall from ours, they are not going to catch us at much. "The guys," as we all so casually call them, have lived there since November, moving in after the two women who had the room both decided to drop out. Most of us who chose to stick it out have become adept at stealing male quantities of food from the cafeteria in the basement of Sadler Hall. Most of the thirty on our hall take turns. We cover up the noise of their talk and instruments with blasts of Led Zeppelin and J. Geils Band. If there is no strength in numbers, there is, at least, in confusion. John Mayall competing with

Leonard Cohen competing with the Grateful Dead. Allman Brothers winning out over Edgar Winter's White Trash.

In return, the band members help with our personal growth. My roommate and I have even learned to eat the worms in the tequila bottles. We don't chew, but we do down the hatch. I mean, we are cool. We are good friends. Forever and all that. We are also probably the only virgins left on the hall, and we are not cool enough to be embarrassed into silence by that fact. We are in no hurry yet.

On a normal Saturday afternoon there's usually no trouble finding something to do, but this very still Saturday afternoon there's no place we want to go and nothing we can think of that we want to do. A lot of people have ditched out for the weekend. Our band is playing a gig in Albany. Nothing's happening on campus except Clint Eastwood and Hill El. Always the independent thinker, I have boycotted the former. My roommate, free at last, boycotts the latter. There's nothing to do but open our books and study, but it's Saturday, and Saturdays, sacred as they are, we feel are better spent hanging out on our cots, contemplating astral projection and the life and love lines on our palms, spouting geysers of smoke like Old Faithful does steam, discussing people's auras as if we can really see them, listening to Leon Russell and Pure Prairie League, to Sandy Denny and Gary Burton, and talking as if we *really* know it all. I mean, like, *really*. We are wise. So wise. We are also, at 3:30 on this particular Saturday afternoon, a little fucked up.

So of course, in the hall beyond our dorm room door, the Sadler Floor 1 phone shrills. Usually, as the ones who live in the room next to the phone, we get stuck answering. But recently we've rebelled. We aren't, after all, in college to become our dormmates' answering service. And right now, today, we don't want to move. We say with bravado to the ceiling, "*Fuck it! Fuck them!*" as only two semi-drunk, nouveau-nicotined virgins can say on a sunny late April afternoon. Spring is just beginning to green the tips of the grass in the field beyond our dorm room window and tint the wine-red flowering Judas buds and the pale fern-green shadow of minute leafing on the trees that mark the far side of the field and the beginning of the wooded, ancient graveyard which curls around two sides of Syracuse's campus.

Amy throws open our door without knocking. "Phone for you, Betsy," she announces and then leaves as quickly, slamming the door.

"We shoulda locked it," my roommate sighs, pouting smoke rings towards the water-stained ceiling. "She is *such a bitch.*"

I rise, with a little stagger, take a cigarette from the turquoise and white Newports pack, and light it as I walk slowly from the room. Not only have I learned to smoke, I can light a cigarette in the middle of Sadler Field in a thirty-mile-per-hour winter wind. I am a wonder. "Yeah," I say, closing the door behind me.

It could be Chris or Richie or Toad. But it's my mother. Saturday afternoon. A time she would never call unless she had to. And she's crying. Clear when she speaks, but crying. It's my grandmother. She's dead. It's a serious phone call, and the Tyrolia fights me for self control. I ask, articulating carefully, "How did she die, Mom?" My mother does not speak for what seems a long time. She is sobbing. I don't know what to say. It seems to me that there should be a prepackaged set of appropriate responses and emotions with which to internalize this news and embrace her obvious distress, but I can't locate it in my repertoire of responses. So I ask again, carefully, "How did she die, Mom?"

I had not thought of my grandmother dying. She was certainly old enough, and she'd been ill in some nonspecific ways. But dead. That makes me want to cry too, not necessarily because I love her, loved her, but I was believing, after nineteen years of trying like crazy to rise above my errors and once and for all get in harmony with her, I was believing that we were making progress. I mean, the last three years my mom has taken me with her when she returned from Pennsylvania to visit her mother. Once a month at least Mom made this drive, and I would go along because she was afraid of I-95, but she took it to get the down-and-back over with as fast as possible. Recently, my grandmother has been confiding in me about her life as a young woman, about the tragedy of love. I think she has been telling me things even my Mom does not know. And now she's dead. "How did she die Mom?"

In my most recent visits, my grandmother has told me over and over about certain moments in her past, particularly about the only boy she really loved. He shot himself in the woods. I imagine deep sapling woods with eerie sunlight splintering here and there, flickering, dappled shade. I imagine the boy (as Jon Voigt) slender, his face looking upward, his eyes pinched closed with emotional distress. His back against a thin trunk, he slips down the tree to sit, knees pulled to chest, forehead pressed to knees, golden streaks in hair slightly long, glinting precious in the fragments of sun, till finally — tears tracking through the dust on his cheeks, the dust from getting there to that tree to that seat — till finally, he pulls a derringer, silver, from his jacket pocket and with unreasonable calm puts the muzzle to his temple and and there I stop imagining until

I imagine her, young and graceful, dressed in organdy, gauzy, long-skirted, coming out to investigate the shot. Who knows how it really happened?

My grandmother tells this story in tandem with the story she tells about meeting my grandfather at a swimming party, off someone's cruising boat in the Chesapeake. He caught her underwater and kissed her. *"Oh that man. That sassy awful man."* He kissed without asking. He stole her kiss. And somehow she ended up married to him. She always tells me these two stories as though she never loved my grandfather, which I know is hard to do, but he was there and her true love was dead. Still, I cannot make the connection, figure how one man led to the next. I *can* imagine the long white dress and her horror in the woods, but I can*not* imagine her A) as a girl in a bathing suit, B) diving off someone's yacht, C) swimming so competently, so fluently that she would be underwater to be caught. Someday I will ask my mother about this, but not now. She is on the other end of a wire, crying. "How did she die, Mom?"

In these recent visits my grandmother has invited me to feel her bones. She is particularly impressed that she herself can feel her ribs and her hip points. It's not that she was ever fat in my memory, though it took a lot of fat for kids to notice fat in my day. But I guess like most adults she has been, well, padded. Midriff bulge. *"If you can squeeze an inch . . ."* Feeling her bones has been one of those things I don't want anyone to know about. Scary. Even, well, sort of unclean in some way. But after our history of natural and spontaneous antagonism I find myself willing to prostitute myself in this way, running my finger over the ridges of ribs, *"Yes, Grandmommy, yes. I can feel the ribs real well. They are real sharp."* Pressing my fingers down on the points of hip bone where they jut out evenly, pulling her crepe skin too snug across them. *"Yes, I can, yes, I can feel your hip bones."* Perhaps it is the darkened rooms of her house, but when I go out to the kitchen where Mom fixes casseroles and other meals easily thawed and cooked for dinners, I have been embarrassed. Embarrassed the way I'd feel coming home from a date and sensing that, whether it was true or not, my parents silently assumed I'd been necking.

My roommate comes out of our room with a tea mug full of Tyrolia. I take it, not wanting it, not drinking it. Back in our room, she cranks my old suitcase stereo and Leon Russell howls about being up on a tight wire — on one side's ice, the other fire." I pour the wine out of the open window that slants inward by the phone, watching Tyrolia dribble in yellow streams down the slanted glass. My cigarette butt follows. On the phone with my mom, with home, I revert to the decent girl I was in August when they left me at a dorm six hours from home. I am suddenly younger, less sure of the day, of my role in it, and I feel sharply that I want to be there, crawl into the phone, slip through the wire. Be *there.* My mother's grief makes me rue the day that I went so far from home to see the world, particularly on a day like today when I ponder that world through smoke and cheap wine, looking for inspiration in the squares of our pressed acoustic tile dorm room ceiling.

"Your grandfather threw her African violet through the dining room window." I hear her gasp through tears. Enraged. Her tears are mixed, sorrow and fury. Ice and fire.

Carefully now I ask, "Through the window? But how come?" Then I ask, "How did that make her die?" Not the right question perhaps. It seems cold, but I need to understand, to get at the logic of it. Why would anyone want to throw African violets through a dining room window and why was that a fatal thing for him to have done, so far as my grandmother is — no was — concerned?

"Because she loved them," my mother says, as if I should know that. But then, I guess I do. He broke her heart. I suspect he had been doing that, one way or another, for a long time.

My grandmother and I had what I named, by the time I was twelve, *The African Violet Wars*, though after the early battles, the violets were involved more symbolically than actually. But the wars began with those violets, those Tanganyikan, now Tanzanian, velvet-leafed plants of such delicate beauty, plants that either punished their tenders for too little or too much, be it light, moisture, food or humidity or else rewarded the same with endless profusions of flowers year-round. Those flowers, so many colors and complexities, their lustrous glimmer of silver specks and veins.

Regardless of the nature of my immediate assaults against the realm of peaceful grandmotherlyhood, my grandmother invoked the violets and their ghosts each time I drove her, however inadvertently, to listing my misdeeds against her realm, as if the violets and my abuses thereof explained my more varied and numerous crimes as I grew towards adolescence. All of my life, all of my mother's life, my grandmother cultivated an impressive collection of violets, many shades from white to midnight violet, indigo, swirling mixtures of color, leaves soft as new chicks. The violets grew and bloomed on the wide ledge of the deep bay window in her dining room. When I was ledge height, I saw them as a cloud of pinks and blues and purples, whites and deep greens. At first it was enough just to look up through the forest of violets out the window to blue sky. Next it was enough to learn who each was. Each violet had a fancy name and most had a history — Gisela, Dominica, Monique and Decennie, Strike Me Pink, Double Pink, Fringed Snow Prince, Blue Pom, Purple Ruffles, Midnight Star, and magically so on. Even then I knew the violets were far more than plants in pots, and after a while, it was no longer enough just to look and know who was who. I couldn't keep my hands where they belonged. I loved to finger those leaves, thick and firm, silky. My grandmother and mother plucked flowers, so I did too, just not the dried up brown ones.

I loved the many different pots, crowded together for maximum profusion. Whether terra cotta or ceramic, large or small, all the pots had watering holes. I learned early on that African Violets, unlike backyard violets, did not like water to touch their furry leaves. *"Those holes aren't for you to put your fingers in, Betsy! And don't touch those leaves! They don't like your fingers anymore than they like water!"* But the holes fit so well. And touching the leaves was like touching the incredibly soft muzzle of a horse. It was inevitable, though, that my fingers would find a hole that was a bit too snug. It was as inevitable too that that particular hole would be in the pot of the oldest and most royal of the violets, a plant passed from generation to generation through carefully nurtured cuttings for so long that it was a plant that went further back than civilization, that it was, perhaps, the original African Violet.

And it was inevitable that, stuck, my efforts to withdraw my finger before anyone caught it where it had no business being would result in the most heinous murder of the best and the oldest. The shattering of its ancient porcelain pot *"My mother's mother's mother's mother's"* was as loud as any death scream. White petals, brown earth, and peach porcelain fragments covered the floor and the murderer as telltale as blood. The shards and slivers my grandmother cleaned away in tears. The rest was left to me, six and humbled, but not so humbled that I did not hide velvet leaves in my pants pocket whenever my grandmother directed her anger in my mother's direction. *"What are you going to do with this child? She is just impossible."*

I realized later that the plant could have been salvaged, if not largely whole, then at least in part. Much later, I could label my grandmother's refusal to do so as a temper fit, one she probably regretted. But then, the leaves in my pocket I handed over in guilt to my mother, who asked me far more gently, *"What are we going to do with you, Betsy?"* and then turned what leaves she could into cuttings. Cuttings. But the plant itself went into the compost pile and withered accusingly at me and my evening offerings for days until a cold snap hit and it died a black twisted death. I remember little terra cotta pots lining the sills of our kitchen as my mother began the next generation of this violet. That story of its loss became one my grandmother told almost every time someone commented on her violets. I knew it by heart. And perhaps that is why I think of all of the various strife between my grandmother and me as our African Violet Wars. In truth, there were only so many things one child could inadvertently do to African violets, and thus the crimes I recall that dealt direct blows to her violets are few.

When I hit the beginning of that age when many grandchildren lose some of their charm for grandparents, someone gave her a violet called a Betsy Bee. I took this addition personally. I thought it might be a sign of her forgiveness. For a while, I even thought she had named it or renamed it after me. My grandmother got this violet the year I could not be good to save myself. I was nine going on ten and could not stay out of trouble no matter how hard I tried, and I did try, particularly where my grandmother was concerned. I truly did try, but nine, for me, was an age when my attention span only allowed me to process the first half of any sentence. I became semi-deaf in some odd way. Like "Betsy, I want you to go to Gossman's and get a stick of butter *synapse but I don't want you taking your bike beyond Benfield Road.*" Or "Betsy, yes, you can clean out the fireplace *synapse but wait till your father and I get back and the coals are completely out.*" I missed the conditional so often and got caught missing that conditional so often that each day I promised myself that I would be careful, listen, make sure. But I could never seem to carry through. My mother, realizing she needed something more than a stick of butter, would in all innocence follow my route to Gossman's Grocery only to find my bike leaning against the stucco wall. My parents, after a Saturday matinee in Annapolis, came home just as the smoldering coals caught and flames flared in my arms, just in time to help me get the grocery bag of fireplace ash out of the house with minimal damage. These things happened every day. It was that kind of year, a bad one.

It was the year I named my favorite plastic horse Louise only to find out that Louise was my grandmother's middle name and that she was not as flattered as I was by the Betsy Bee. It was the year I tried adult psychology, child version, on my mother and told her that if she did not get me a blow-up raft, all of the people at the beach would think she was mean. It was the year that my friends Tommy and Matt and I found this wrecked car down over a cliff and, with a crow's appreciation for the brighter things in life, stuffed the shattered safety glass from the windshield in our pants pockets, hoarding it like jewels. Safety is relative, though, and by the time we biked the three or four miles home, we had odd and nasty little cuts wherever the front and back pockets of our pants pressed against our bodies — more of a problem for Matt and Tommy than me. It was also the year that they dared me to bike the tennis courts at Severn School for Boys as though the net poles were barrels in a quarter horse neck-reining competition. I caught my right biceps on a nct pole, split my arm open and we had to come up with some convincing lie before they would let me go home to get fixed. They told me to say that a car had just tapped the back wheel of my bike and thrown me into a hug with a telephone pole. *"It is the only other way it could have happened,"* they said. None of us was old enough, aware enough, to know that for a car to tap a bike and then proceed on its way was a serious crime. We did not know that a telephone pole would leave a different sort of gash and a more extensive one at that. We did not know the kinds of questions parents can think up that make a lie harder and harder to hold on to.

It was also the year when I realized that my friend Charlie's older brother was always on crutches and that his speech was never quiet clear, and when I asked his mother what was wrong with him, *he* answered and said, "I had polio." It was the year when we first filed into a building at the Severn School for Boys and ate sugar cubes, red with sweet polio vaccine that had come too late for Hugh. It was the year my cousin Tim threatened, his pen knife open and pressing plastic, the blow-up raft that my mother had finally bought me and I bit him, blackmailing through clenched jaw, *"Throw the knife away. Throw the knife away."* I clenched, a pit bull with a cause. He pressed the shiny steel blade closer and into the tender royal blue plastic. I clenched deeper, drawing blood, tasting its salt. Adults came from everywhere when he screamed. I jerked my teeth from his upper arm, startled as if by sudden bright light. Blood dripped down my chin from my teeth and my lower lip and he, the angel, the saint, the perfect boy, the only grandson, was quickly coddled back to my grandparents' house and kept away from me, the heathen, the vicious child, the *"what's wrong with that girl?"* girl. Later he told me he had had to have a tetanus shot, that his doctor said there was no mouth on earth dirtier than a human mouth, *"particularly a girl's mouth."* I believed him and felt more bad and soiled than usual.

Ah, bad girl. It was the year when our parakeet, Peter the Parakeet, took to leaving his perennially open cage at dinner time and landing by my plate, near the green beans or corn or black-eyed peas, muttering, *"Dirty Betsy. Dirty Betsy. Bad Betsy. Shut up Betsy. Bad Betsy."* Peter would move from the tablecloth to the edge of my plate, cursing me under his breath as he went, and no one but me quite heard what he said in these intimate moments, though he was not shy about squawking his insults across the room. My sisters would look on with envy at his attention to me. I would wonder later who taught him these curses. I would suspect my older sister, and I would suspect my grandmother. My mother says she does not know.

But then, it just seemed he spoke the truth. Ah, bad and clumsy girl. I sank the skiff. I got stranded twice across the river in the sailing canoe even though my mother said she had told me not to cross the river. It was the year, fascinated by the myth of Icarus, that I took to making wings and pilot testing them on Matt. It was the year I led Tommy along a short cut I'd found through the Round Bay woods to go soft crabbing. I jumped a few feet down to a big log and he followed and the log was teeming with yellow jackets. I got bitten thirty-six times. He got eighteen bites. I was sore, but hardy. He was allergic and nearly died. I got him home somehow, and he got what he needed not to die, but I, the villain, the ruffian, the *"What's-with-you-girl?"* girl was not allowed near him for a year. By then, he was beginning to hate girls anyway, though he and his friend would play with them if they would take their shirts off, and that was no fun. Besides, in the intervening year of solitude, while Tommy's housekeeper forgot the bees and Matt's broken arm healed well, I learned to enjoy my time with myself.

But it was one of those years when nothing goes right, not even school. It was a year when, as usual, I got straight As, but I also quite effectively dripped poster paints down Oswald W.'s back during a film. He was always trying to grab me, kiss me when the teacher turned out the lights for movies or something, but she always made us sit together and in the back because we were a good head taller than most of our peers. "Sprouting like field corn," Doc Doolin the janitor would say when we walked by.

One afternoon in our darkened classroom, when Oswald W. put his arm over my shoulders and pulled me against him, I acted on good womanly instinct. I tenderly touched his back for the rest of the film, stroking it gently with poster paints from the quart jars behind us on the art table. There was no question as to who'd done it. And my motive was not of interest to my teacher or the principal. Under Mrs. Parson's glare, I wrote a letter to his mother apologizing for damaging his shirt and promising to replace it if the paint wouldn't wash out. I used the word "unsalvageable" several times because Mrs. Parson, in an effort to make the letter writing a learning experience, gave me five words to use — one word was "unsalvageable." Another was "unforgivable." My P.S. (I always added at least one P.S. to every letter I wrote) read, "But he always tries to kiss me when the lights are out for movies and I hate him." My teacher let that pass through. I don't think she really read the finished letter carefully, and I'd put the P.S. on the back of the last page. To bring closure to her punishment, I was the one who sealed the confession in its envelope which she'd addressed. Then she marched me to a corner mailbox and watched me mail it. I think that was the first time I felt the finality of the slam of a letter box in the pit of my stomach.

At Oswald's school birthday party a few months later, his mom ruffled the hair on the top of my head when she found out who I was. She said, "You gotta paint 'em as you see 'em, hon. It came out easy. Water soluble." *Water soluble.* I can't say I understood then, but I still remember her sharply — thin, tight jeans, gauze shirt, long black hair, *Indian* I thought. *Cherokee.*

I just couldn't recognize trouble when I saw it. Life was an unposted mine field across which I joyfully danced, explosions all around, never understanding what had happened or why. Piaget or Vygotsky must describe some stage involving this phenomenon of not understanding the connectedness of thought to action, of action to response, of response to social sanction. I left third grade with a bad reputation. It was the year I spent most of the recesses either hiding up in the maple in the first grade playground or in the dense and tall pine in the main playground. The recess teachers would find me, stand below and call me down as if they'd never climbed a tree. I only came down when the recess teachers invoked Mrs. Baylus, matron of the Safeties. For my last three years of grade school Safeties called out, rather with the same tone as our parakeet, the dreaded summons, *"Three-thirty Monday, Betsy,"* announcing to anyone in earshot that I was a trouble-maker, a rule-breaker, a bad girl.

I did not understand the teachers. I did not understand why I could not travel my own way home without waiting for the Safety Crossing when between the hours of 3 P.M. and 8 A.M. and on weekends I crossed the same road on my own. I did not understand a lot. I did not understand my grandmother, and she did not seem to particularly understand or like me.

And now she is dead. My mother has handed the phone to my father and I am arranging with him how I should get home, my first plane flight.

The odd thing is, I am a lot like my grandmother. But I am also a lot like her sister with whom my grandmother fought whenever proximity allowed it. Perhaps I am the nexus of them, the point of their conflict. I look back twenty-one years now to that me who sat on my dorm cot, my roommate gone for breakfast, my duffle packed, waiting for the desk to buzz my room, a signal that the cab had arrived to ferry me to the airport. And I wish. I wish. I don't know. I guess I wish my grandmother and I had been close, had loved each other and I'd known it. No, I wish we had *liked* each other and been at ease with each other. There's a ubiquitous song from grade school *"Over the river and through the woods to Grandmother's house we go. The horse knows the way, to pull the sleigh, across the blanket of snow."* My grandmother lived right beside me until I was fourteen. My grandmother did not have a wood stove, round cherry cheeks, or a fat silver bun. My grandmother was probably too close to her only daughter's children, all of us, to see us the same way she saw the cousins who lived an hour away. And while my older sister was turning into a young woman of marriageable age, thus interesting, and my younger sister was a toddler, cute and precocious, I just *was* — big for my age, clumsy, blunt cut straight hair, styleless.

She saw me more than enough every day and found me frustrating. I read too much. I was not interested in womanly interests — refused to learn to knit, to sew, to crochet, to do needlepoint. I was interested in sharks pianos snakes cellos horses blue claw crabs Mozart China math muskmelons *National Geographics* all wild animals cats dreams school college oceanography writing. I was going to be a doctor who made it so no one died and an oceanographer who explored the Mariana Trench (with dolphins), a concert pianist and a jockey, a world traveler and an essayist and a large-animal vet. I was going to ride in the Olympics and win the Kentucky Derby. My heroes were Nancy Drew and Alec Ramsey and Robin Hood and Fess Parker and Amelia Earhart. And I was never going to marry, but if I had to, I'd have two sets of identical twins — first girls, then boys. And I would have my own house, he his. These things I knew for sure by the time I was ten going on eleven.

"The girl spends too much time in fantasy worlds." When she caught me spread eagle in the field of yard behind my house, trying to transport my essence through the earth to trade places with a counterpart, a kindred spirit I was sure existed in China, she threw up her hands, particularly when she found out the counterpart was a boy my age. We would just trade bodies and languages, just for a little while, a few days perhaps, to see each other's homes and schools. I could imagine this earth journey

so clearly, my essence spread-eagled, moving steadily through rock and roots and rabbit warrens. My inner-earth vision was drawn right from Alice's middle-earth adventures. My interest in China was motivated by pieces of oriental sounding music my piano teacher had me playing and by mementos passed down to my mother by her great Aunt Fan, the deaf spinster and world traveler. And the boy part — well boys got around more, and I was sure it was worse to be a girl in China where their feet were bound and stayed so tiny that they couldn't move fast if they had to.

When my grandmother first got the Betsy Bee African violet, I was charmed. I took it as an unspoken apology on her part. It was not much of a violet, really, a faded lavender with lighter than usual leaves. But its name was my name. I mean, she couldn't come right out and tell me that she was sorry she'd disliked me all these years, could she? Doing so, she would have to admit the fact, and since grandmothers should only love grandchildren, going public with her dislike would have been risking too much. As it was, only she and I knew. I asked my mother once why my grandmother did not like me and my mother said I was mistaken. My father said that my grandmother had had a hard life and was tired and angry, but not at me. My older sister told me it was because no one liked children until they reached fifteen. Then they began to become people.

The Betsy Bee was, for some reason, proof to me that she had, in fact, disliked me and things were going to get better. And I was more than willing to help things get better. I remember being suffused with a kind of passion for my grandmother that truly was not unlike the kind of passion I would feel for my first serious boyfriend eight years later. Both she and he had a common problem with me, actually: *"Don't tell me you love me! Show me!"* For a while, I snuck the violet extra water, but it soon showed unmistakable signs of drowning. My culpability obvious, I received a lecture on African violets, their need for water, carefully administered. I promised not to water it and later snuck it outside to dry out, forgot it, and nearly fried it. Once it recovered, owing nothing to me, I picked some blooms and gave them to my grandmother — a miniature bouquet. I crept up behind her as she vacuumed, extended the hand that held the bouquet, and cried out, "Boo!"

As I flushed her toilet the blossoms swirled down in a purple spiral. My cheek smarted from the palm of her hand. The Betsy Bee was not named after me, she said. *"It is a very regular-looking violet. Clara the ironing woman gave it to me. She crossed to get it. sometimes you cross and get a good one, sometimes not. This one is alright, just alright."*

By the time we moved to Pennsylvania and I was making regular trips back to Maryland with my mother, my sister's prophecy had seemingly proved true. At fifteen, though I was not her favorite, my grandmother did not dislike me. She began to tell me her stories, stories she'd only told my mother, if anyone — about the boy she loved, about the husband she may not have loved, about her dreams put off too long, but never forgotten. But in a very real way, nothing was ever resolved between us. I have been left on my own to reconcile our differences, and I have given up believing in miracles of any kind or in momentous changes in people's ways of seeing. I know there can only be resolution among me and the selves I have been and will be along my way.

In the end, it is I who have needed to love that Betsy who was incurably blunt, who stepped on Janie Gregor's mother's minute, fragile foot and broke two bones, who dreamed and forgot, who could not stay out of trouble in spite of herself. Some memories like razors remain sharp, making cuttings deep and long lasting. But then, African violets stem from cuttings, leaves that slipped gently into soil and watered, survive when one bit of growth takes up the soil as its home and sends up a shoot. And it is through the crossing of plants that the original two have produced thousands of varietals, hybrids and mutants which promise even greater numbers as time goes on. They are wounded before they can become grown and blooming. They are valued for their histories and for their futures.

Learning to Name

All truths being multiple, it is not surprising that the true version of any story is also multiple.

Wendy Doniger O'Flaherty,
Other People's Myths

In learning to name was I really any wiser?

Reg Saner,
The Four-Cornered Falcon

What
the River
Meant

In prior lives I was a bird and a horse and a sea mammal. When of the air, I was a great blue heron, powerful of wing, sharp of eye, unwavering in patience. When of the ground, I was Pegasus and with winged agility jumped large obstacles in my path. When of the sea I was a porpoise, playful and wise, a saver of the drowning. In this life, like the porpoise, I have always swum fluidly, instinctively, always courting the uplifting viscosity of water and grateful for the buoyant me it created. My body of water, the Severn River, defined me from our first contact, updating its mold of me each time I slipped into its depths or followed its shores. The river shaped me to fit its curves and bays. It sharpened my senses till I could perceive its most minor nuances of current and salinity, hints of hidden sources, a cold pool surrounded by warm July river, indicating a spring of fresh water easing into the river from somewhere underground, helping the salt at its mouth lessen to brack water and finally to fresh. The Severn was the perfect mentor for one open to its lessons, be they of baited hooks and waiting, of swamps and muskrats, cottonmouths and snappers — lessons in naming and predicting, lessons in surviving the threats of electric storms and eccentric people. I was the perfect student and in any season the Severn was my passion. The river was mine.

My first summer love was a Mr. Roberts. During the school year he taught in some capacity, I think at the Naval Academy, nine miles down the Severn from us. But during the summers, when I was three, four, five, six, he taught swimming at the public beach near my home. I believe he was the lifeguard as well — a strong mature man who would be followed, after the summer he never returned, not by men, but by big boys, eighteen or nineteen, who drew girls like, well, like ripe blackberries draw turtles, like dead fish on the shore draw vultures, like swimmers in motion draw sea nettles, like winter flocks of migrating swans, in their silent silver glinting chevrons, drew my mother and me down to the river with holy offerings of stale bread and cookies.

When these boys replaced Mr. Roberts, the deep end of the long, long community pier became, increasingly, a social club, so much so that the end of the pier had to be expanded to accommodate the times — teens in bikinis, loud AM radios rickety with static, boys in Boston Whalers and other outboards whipping up to the pier into abrupt stops to pick up bikinied passengers, the crest of the fifties and the beginning of the sixties. Our pier, and the river even, became in a sense bicultural. For those steeped in traditions of hunting and gathering, the river was a respected place of daily routines that demanded honed skills. Along the length of many piers that reached out into the river, small to medium boats were tied up, stern and bow hitched to pilings and pier. These were the boats of the traditionalists. If one did not arrive at the piers before mid-morning one might believe that the boats never left. But they did, daily and with purpose. For those who had not taken up those traditions, the river was a playground — a place of speed, competition, and recklessness. Fast boats, fast swimmers, fast boys, fast love.

The ends of the community piers that reached into the river from Linstead, Round Bay, Sherwood Forest and else-where were decorated by taut and vital youth. As the end of our pier grew more social, it grew unsafe in several ways. Most obviously, the carpet of towels and bodies made it hard to get to ladders and dives. Any serious swimmer or diver was always in the awkward position of stepping over and around torsos, of dripping cool water on dry, Coppertoned legs and playing cards, of being treated to the practicing tongue of a potential shrew. If one was a kid, like me, or an older girl who was shy and not easily social, like my older sister, the end of the pier was fraught with emotional dangers — open curiosity, mockery, rejection, and indifference. Eventually someone got the idea to paint a freeway, no beach towels or loungers' painted toenails allowed. The white painted footprints marked access to all ladders, to low and high dives, to the designated swimming areas enclosed in useless but symbolic sea nettle nets, to the lifeguard stand. Girls could carpet the rest of the pier's end with their crazy quilt of clashing vivid towels made three-dimensional by browning, two-pieced bodies and numer-ous games of Hearts. It was quite a sight to see from above. I know, because one of my favorite of the big boy lifeguards, Dean, used to ask *me* to mind the lifeguard seat when he would break his vigil and dive elegantly from his perch to cool off in the dark Severn waters.

He would rise, suddenly, stretch his arms up, back, out, and then with a powerful thrust fly up into an arc. From that apex, like a royal tern or an osprey or an eagle, he'd plummet straight and long down into the water and enter without a splash. Somehow he always seemed to move in agonizingly slow motion; all the girls on their towels would look up from their cards and freeze, watching him raptly, raw awe on their faces, as if he were some meteor or space capsule descending to earth. What I saw was Dean doing a good dive and leaving his perch to me. I wondered what those girls saw.

Mr. Roberts, the predecessor of these boys, did not soar to the attention of girls, defying gravity with graceful beauty. Instead, he gave that defiance and grace to his swimmers. I remember him standing on the east side of the pier with me or some other young one *standing* on his flattened, upturned hands, hands larger than our own feet. Our soft soles molded themselves to the firm mounds of his palms — of his Moon and Sun, of his Venus. Our heels secured themselves along his palms' life lines. Finally he would gently but with gathering speed heft us up and launch us toward the sky. It was always our choice whether to descend head first or feet first, but for me, at the peak of that momentary flight, my body always curled forward into a straight down dive into the lapping waters. And Mr. Roberts always clapped and called out, "Good Betsy. Good!"

I fell in love with Mr. Roberts because he gave me flight. I loved the perfect fit of my soles into the mystical geography of his palms. I loved the boundless joy I felt when he launched me into the sky. I loved the boundless joy I saw on the faces of his other swimmers. He did not force flight, like some adults would, on those among us who did not feel the joy. Our joy was his and his time with us was spent on us. He did not dive for us in demonstration or show. In fact, I never saw him dive at all. Like the boats that were stabled along the pier, and like the people who gathered sustenance from the river, Mr. Roberts was of tradition. Because of him and some others, I early on made a choice to value the traditions of the river — the ropes that would swing us high out over the water, the search for every best place to swim, for every hidden cove and beach, the learning and relearning of the lines of the shores, following the runs of muskrats and tracks of raccoons through the swamps, the smell of water moccasins, the recording in memory of something loved that was bound to change. Hot white sun of summer days. Cool water on sun-blushed skin.

Later, when Mr. Roberts was gone and Dean took his perch, I was accused of being in love with Dean, but he really was too young for me. My bond to him was simply rooted a mutual appreciation for the glory of flight, the love of water, and the fact that I was the one who got to sit high in his perch when he vacated it. From nine feet up even the biggest and meanest of the older girls became almost indistinguishable from one another, like gulls in a flock. Like gulls too, the girls' loud talk, rollicking calls to one another, lost their meaning in the confusion of their many voices and the scratch of AM transistor radios straining to pull coherent sounds of music all the way from Baltimore. Together, nine feet below me, the girls became a crowd of giggling and frivolous colors. They rarely if ever went into the water. They rarely if ever fished or crabbed. They went out in boats, but most often the speed boats driven by fast boys. One or two of the girls could water ski well, but most preferred to sit on the bows of boats and glamorously lean back against the windshields, the wind of speed blowing long hair into fuzzy knots. I knew from experience that this was not a pleasant place to ride. The sharp spray strikes bare skin like miniature lances. But the girls looked good and knew so. I eventually grew self-conscious of some part of me that was curious about Hearts and glamour, about looking good. With this recognition came an understanding of why the girls flocked on the end of the pier instead of lying on the softer and more comfortable beach with the mothers and toddlers. Their work for the summer *was* to look good. My work was different. I had long before cast my lot with the traditionalists, and I could not take the time to sit and, well, learn to chatter and watch boys and play cards. To do so, I thought then, would waste time. I could never figure out was how anyone could live on the river and not become a part of the river. I was judgmental, yes, wondering what a river was for if one did not partake of it in as many ways possible. But I never learned to play Hearts. I never did learn to play Hearts.

The only time in my life that I truly hated my parents was when they moved us from the Severn River to Pennsylvania, an hour from downtown Philadelphia. It was not that there were not beauty and space; our house backed up into the wooded edge of a state park and a convent property, neither of which would ever be developed. But woods by themselves did not seem so special then. All that mattered then was that there was no river, that the only water nearby was a creek, at most twenty feet wide, which ran through the state park, until it eventually disappeared altogether, retreating back underground and,

after that, evident only where a controlled gush of its water surfaced through pipes to pour into the trough of an artesian well.
In this creek there was one place deep enough to be a good
swimming hole, but there was also a park warden whose sole
job, in the summer, seemed to be keeping kids out of that
swimming hole and well-monitored in the dark pine forests,
out of the trouble he imagined us getting into. I mourned my
loss of the Severn River for years, but particularly that first year
when, in unfamiliar terrain and lacking the basic teenage social
skills, I lived housebound as well as landlocked. Leaving the
river behind meant leaving myself. As I figure it now, my life
until this move had split three ways: a third to school and reading and music, a third to my adults, and a third to the river. And
it was from the river I got the most natural and honest defini-
tions of me. It was from the river that I most learned about
myself. One cannot have one third of one's life's devotion dis-
placed without serious loss, serious change. I lost my spirits and
my rules. I lost the things I did best outside of school.

I lost some crucial roles that defined me — explorer,
hunter and gatherer, family provider. For me and some others,
the river meant a real and valued source of food, food we understood and respected and protected. When we fished we
never took more than we needed and we used the whole fish.
Body to the table, head and guts to the vegetable garden. We
knew where the fish were almost as well as they did themselves.
We knew the days and the times of day when they would
ignore our bait and when they would be waiting. But even
more, we moved to the rhythms of the crabbing season, beginning with the flowering of locust trees and waning with the closing of September, marked by full moons when the crabs were
at their best, full and fat and ready to shed their current shells

for the next size up — yet the crab was more than dinner. Its spirit and cunning made catching it an art. We were religious about the rules of the catch — no traps, only lines and chicken necks and hand-guided nets. No female crabs allowed in the steamer — if crabs cultivated a worshipful following, they cultivated, too, a rich awareness of the importance of a matriarchal society. It's not only that the female crab is not as delectable as the male, but she more than any creature I have known illustrates how crucial females are to the survival of life. One mature female crab, a sook, can produce nearly two million eggs, but the fates of these eggs are many. If it is true, as believed, that for every million only one or two eggs make it to adulthood, therein lies the logic behind a rule that protects her. A good Jimmy will be increasingly hard to find if the she-crab is sacrificed to the pot and not her young.

Logic too informs the rule that there shall be no keeping of any crab not five good inches point to point. Not only are the smaller crabs hard and sharp to pick, but without some restrictions all crabs would be at the mercy of human greed and gluttony. All of these rules might as well have been on the books, as some were. They were definitely in our hearts. We did not need them to be official, for respecting the crab meant not only taking just what we needed; it meant taking it only when available naturally. No dredging in off season.

When I say that the river created me, defined me, I know I sound melodramatic. But I would be someone else, someone absolutely different, some person I cannot at all imagine, had the Severn not been, for my first fourteen and a half years, my domain and companion. I spent most of my time on it quite alone and yet never alone. In a canoe cutting silently across the glass that is the river at dawn, I was completely with myself in a way which always went beyond the physical. In that sense, the river and my freedom on it gave me a developed sense of self that would always exist to reassert itself, no matter how sorely I would treat it, how little I would value it at times, how easily I would, in the future, set that self aside to meet the demands of love or friendship, of school or job.

There were many things a kid could do with a river, and likewise in return. Rivers are not just there for our uses. They are entities unto themselves, laced into every aspect of the land and life around them. They have deep-rooted and timeless lessons to offer those who will listen and see. Indeed, rivers can teach one how to see and listen. Rivers are the veins of the world, forever flowing through the heart of the matter.

Almost without fail, when a day is planning to be clear, the river in the early morning is motionless. To be the first to slip into its mirroring of sunrise, the first to glide out into deep water, silently slipping a wooden canoe through water, dipping the paddle perfectly, no drips, no splash — to be the first to take possession of the river's incredible morning gifts of beauty was my goal for each day of the summer from the time I was eight. There is no feeling on earth like being eight, ten, twelve, and sliding weightless into the morning, the first person awake. No. The first person on earth. Sometimes I could manage an hour or more before the first engine's roar ripped the air, shattering the silence. With that roar the river immediately would begin to get restless, agitated. It was then that I would go home and do a turn-around, breakfast in hand, to join my grandfather in his daily morning run for fish. It was then the world would shrink as others filled it with their noise and their needs. It was then that I slid back into my role as daughter, granddaughter, sister, and Betsy. I have never felt so all-encompassing, yet so fully encompassed, as on those mornings when I was alone, with the power and the choice to travel miles.

The Severn, like all rivers, was and is a conduit, a highway with no toll booths, an open gate. For me then, the sheer connectedness, endlessness, of that conduit was sublimely frustrating. I can understand why it is that some people have lived for the risk of moving under their own power across oceans. I would have, any summer day, taken up the challenge to see how far I could canoe. To the Chesapeake, to its juncture with the ocean, to France. It seemed so possible. At times, just before turning back, I would still the canoe in the center of the river and look down it, imagining buoys and bridges I could not see, feeling the excitement of what it would mean to surge from the Severn's mouth, alone in this canoe, into the bay.

But then too, just as rivers go down to the sea, they go up to their beginnings. Some glassy mornings I would slide silently up the river. It bent right at ninety degrees around Sandy Point and then bent again ninety degrees left, perhaps a half mile further on, at the inlet to Yantze's Cove. From there, the wide path ran straight for a while, past large houses where rich people lived (one the gracious granite summer home of the owner of Hendlers Ice Cream), past a working marina and stretches of tall pines, till it narrowed and narrowed and narrowed further still, and the canoe would scrape bottom. The nettle bushes growing on both banks would reach out to sting, and the river would go where I could not go without leaving the boat and risking the sorts of dangers that masquerade as sandy bottoms and firm ground. I never made it to the Severn's source, but I often contemplated doing so, and tried doing so, going just a bit further, staying just a bit longer.

The river and its surrounding environment meant the freedom to adventure. Without thinking, from my first boat on,
I went miles away from home. For my eighth birthday my
mother and grandfather built from a kit a wood-frame and
canvas kayak. They built it in the basement on the ping pong
table between Valentine's Day and early April. The trade-off,
not having a birthday party, was no loss. There weren't many
kids around to invite, and the alternatives were always more
interesting and longer lasting anyway. By eight, I knew that
sometime in January my mother would approach me with the
choice, a birthday party or a _____. I always opted for the
_____ and thus never had a birthday party until I was sixteen, and that was the doing of high school friends. All my
mother had to do was get me out of the house for a day while
my friends transformed the basement — hanging crepe paper
and balloons, securing the Twister Game with masking tape,
clearing a space for a dance floor, and setting up the music. I
had spent January waiting for the choice, wondering what the
option would be this year. We were not in the Sweet sixteen car
economic class, but I was not beyond hoping.

It strikes me now how many of my choices were serious
vehicles — the kayak, a rowing skiff, an outboard for that skiff,
a five-speed bike, a Sunfish. The kayak was the first and my
favorite. There is a picture of me standing beside my grandfather, the kayak paddle standing vertical in my hand. When I
think of this picture without seeing it, I always put my mother
into it, for she — as much or more than he — built this boat
for me. But when I come across the picture, she is absent — a
statement on her part. The kayak was to her as the pike was to
me so far as my grandfather was concerned. But still, the picture is rich in the moment.

Clearly the weather is cool. I wear long green corduroy pants and Keds sneakers, a gray cotton jacket over a sweater. My hair is blunt cut two or three inches above the shoulders, parted on the side and pulled back with a barrette. Serviceable hair, wispy and gold from years of sun. My face is full with uncensored smile, no pretty pose. In front of us lies the kayak, red canvas on top and gray canvas stretching over the rest of its compact wooden skeleton. If we had had a home movie camera then, I could have watched myself as I got in and was shoved off the sand into the shallows, where I fumbled the paddle and wobbled as I navigated around the many moored boats. I didn't stay out long that time because kayaking is wet and, in early spring, cold, but before I returned to shore, I had caught on to the grace of the boat. Another photo, taken from the pier, catches me taking a sharp left turn away from the camera, a small clean wake even behind the prow. By summer, however, I was skillful and yakked around the river fearlessly. The river was wide at the point where we lived, and while my parents did not forbid me to cross it, they did ask me to cross at narrow points if I really had to cross. I *did* have to cross the river, just as the bear had to cross the mountain. And I often crossed fast at the widest part, always risking not being seen by one of the large cabin cruisers or fishing boats or one of the many fast boats that were increasingly present on the river. The kayak sat about three inches above the surface of the river. From a distance I must have looked like a person wading chest deep, later, waist deep.

While the river was a place of joy, it was also a place of mystery and danger, the latter mostly borne of human agency.

The river's mysteries were its colors and the changes in its mood, its inhabitants and their seasons, its fish and its crabs, its coves, its nooks and crannies. Any of these mysteries could be made dangerous, but the truth is that someone had to choose to make them so. And people did.

People, young and old, drowned every year. People flipped their boats crossing too fast through a heavy wake or collided with other boaters in a mad dash to win some race or some game of chicken. Boats driven by those who did not know the river well occasionally ran aground on a shallow sand bar, sometimes fast enough to catapult a passenger or so. People ignored the river's warnings and those of the air and sky. People acted without care, diving into too shallow water, going too close to the many possible dangerous edges any river offers. In the winter the river and its bays and coves froze, but rarely so solidly that the ice was safe. Children fell through, sometimes just to face the pain of a long walk home pulling a sled with a cold hand in a frozen mitten, sometimes slipping through the ice and getting lost beneath it until spring. Once a drowning occurred and the body not recovered till a thaw came; before that, even the most solid ice would not tempt some of us back near that spot — not so much because we feared for our own lives so much as we feared finding the victim, frozen and dead, yet staring up at us from that world below the ice.

The sand cliffs that in places cut jaggedly upward, high above the river on its north side lured kids. There were cavities to hide in, exposed roots that served as seats or ropes, gnarled scrub trees to climb as they twisted precariously from the vertical ground; but cliffs collapsed and smothered, roots and trees groaned and shifted and then let go. Warnings sounded. Some people listened, some not. I did both, depending on what I wanted to do. And at times I knew I was lucky to survive. I remember moments from life there and shake my head, but not without knowing that, in part, I am also who I am because of close calls on foolish days. I wonder if all children have close calls with injury and death because they take risks with forces that are larger than they and suspect so.

By the time I was twelve, I was very much aware of another sort of human agency.

Several incidents lurk in my mind in a dark recess with a gaping mouth that collects, in spite of my efforts to forget, atrocities that touch me. Both polluted the river in a spiritual way. The first, the specifics of which I do not at all fully recall, involved alcohol and the crossing of the railroad bridge and college boys. One young man was definitely killed, perhaps two. Someone's sons died because of someone else's ability to make others take risks that common sense should tell them from the start will end their lives. I remember that this incident provoked memories in my adults of a another, earlier event, one before my time, also involving the railroad bridge — a fraternity rite, a young man tied to the tracks in the dark, his brothers fully intending to release him before the 4:30 A.M. train came through. And I am sure they would have, but the night they chose for this rite was the night the 4:30 A.M. train began coming through at 2:30 A.M. A simple change in schedule. This death preceded my consciousness, but the story had become part of the lore of the river and its bridges. The later deaths revived memories of the earlier one. Because the railroad bridge was forbidden ground to us, we were privy to the details of this death as warning, so I thought often about that young man tied to the tracks when the train came, not thinking of his death, the blood, but of his anger and terror in the moments before. His last moments must have been very long. I though often, too, of the boys crossing the bridge and wondered why, given the choice, they had not jumped into the river, though at night that would have meant jumping on faith into profound darkness, trusting that the river was below and deep enough.

Yet another incident, one I was around to share the horror of, raised more issues and caused greater horror in my household and the community. It was hard work, I remember, to find out what had happened, and so this memory is more incomplete. No one would tell me anything. I had to locate and spy on hushed conversations. But I caught enough to construct the event in part, enough to recognize even then that something hideous was going wrong with the world. Someone had opened up two recent graves in an African American cemetery and taken the heads. Whoever was involved took the heads to a party, rolling them through the opening door like bowling balls down a lane. A day or so later, the heads were found floating in the river in a bushel basket, a crabbing basket, as I understood it. A man, said to be fishing off his private pier, saw the basket floating by, half below the water line. He snared it with his boat hook and pulled it to him. An extra crab basket is never wasted. I wonder if he thought someone's basket of shedders had come loose from its tie and that he was getting some unexpected soft crabs for his dinner. I wonder how bad the scent of death was, if there was any warning before he popped the lid off and found the heads. I wonder how ill the sight made him and how coherent he was when he raced into his house, perhaps shoving past his concerned wife, busy in their kitchen, and called the police, sobbing out what he'd found. I know, from his nearest neighbors and from the loop-tape of litany that buzzed in shushes and whispers day after day, that he had stumbled off his pier screaming, calling for his wife, calling to God, stumbling up the cement steps built into the steep bank from the beach and then across his back lawn. Adults shook their heads and said, poor man, that he would never be the same or perhaps that he would never be completely sane. What I wondered then and understood later was that none of us could be the same, even completely sane, after a brush with such madness.

Someone was arrested. I remember his name, and I remember adult heads shaking in disbelief and horror. But though he was the instigator and of voting and drinking age, he wasn't the only one involved. Some involved were minors, some not. At least that was my impression. It was my impression, too, that though this incident also involved some coming of age rite, that involvement was different than in the incidents with the trains. I know it triggered a difficult passage for our extended community of river dwellers, for it marked the end of an era in which the trusted illusion of human goodness and safe harbors was rarely challenged. It marked the dawning of an era when that illusion would be shattered again and again.

I don't recall the exact year, and I probably will never go find out, though it had to be the mid-sixties and I am sure the story lies in several newspaper morgues. But I remember this incident waking me up to a different way of seeing the world, much as my younger sister's sudden and unexpected death would wake me up about thirty years later. Though I had always lived with my share of fears, I could name them — my grandfather, two aunts, an uncle, two cousins, a few teachers, several local boys, certain dogs. This new fear did not name easily. Hatred? Grand Malice? Sickness of Mind? Satanism?

Racism? Human Madness? Utter Impurity of Heart? All of those? I could no longer feel completely comfortable when alone with myself. Part of me always watched over my shoulder, not for anything specific. The freedom of my expansive river grew limited as an eeriness closed in on me, more when I was alone on its shores than on its waters. The sun seemed less bright. Alone, the wind seemed more chill and whistling. Shadows moved in the trees, just at the edge of my peripheral vision. I waded in a hollow realization that something had shifted and gone terribly, terribly wrong. So I began to spend less and less time with myself, and after a while I even relegated to my unconscious the absolute joy of solitude and the river, the pure joy of being alone with myself.

When we moved away from the river and north to Pennsylvania, even though I made clear to my parents that they were destroying my life, I had already begun to be less a part of the river and its environs and, in a sense, less a part of myself. To be alone became a symbolic state demanding symbolic acts — the closing of a bedroom door, the putting on of headphones and the closing of eyes, the acts of anger that could be mistaken as adolescence, but were more from suddenly being penned up. I think we all, my parents and younger sister alike, felt this entrapment, this spiritual dehydration. The river had defined home, had been home. Without it, there was no functioning definition of home. When we moved from the river, we became people we would never have been otherwise, people we could not have remotely imagined, at times people we would never even have wanted to remotely imagine.

Baptism III
Learning to Name

One   My grandmother and I are driving down the Governor
Ritchie Highway toward Annapolis. Just the two of us, we are
heading for Aunt Florence's where she lives on the Magothy
River, so as we near Arnold we turn left off Governor Ritchie
and proceed neatly on the curving back roads in my grandmother's sea green Studebaker, with its swan hood ornament
gliding before us like the pointer of a compass. Aunt Florence
and her husband Ben are old, so I call them aunt and uncle,
even though they are not. In a few years, when I openly and
sincerely name them with these titles, I will receive a confus-
ing litany of relationships of firsts and thirds, once and twice
removed, mechanics and schematics of blood relationships that
will only sink in enough for me to switch from aunt and uncle
to cousin, Cousin Florence, Cousin Ben.

   I did not go to Aunt Florence's often, even though she
lived fewer than ten miles from us on the next river north of

the Severn. She and Uncle Ben had no children, if I recall correctly, and their house was small. I never felt welcomed there, but it was nothing personal, just that any child there was to be silent and invisible while the adults did their visiting. I went there infrequently, and when I did, I had always changed enough to merit reintroduction. I remember Aunt Florence very little, just a small woman with a short cap of curly, almost fuzzy white hair, and I remember her house only from the outside and then only from the back yard where I was supposed to stay so as not to wander onto the road and risk getting hit by a car.

The room at the back of her house had many small-pane windows — perhaps a closed-in porch, perhaps a kitchen — and I remember ceramic objects and the flowers. Probably African Violets. Put out the back door like a cat, facing the Magothy River, my back to the house, I would stand and see to the right a large tree with a tempting swing made up of a round of wood dangling from thick rope that went through a center hole bored through the round seat and knotted underneath. To get to the swing I had to get around a huge billy goat on a chain anchored by a strong iron stake. The goat was white and for many years taller than I. He had backwards curving horns, hard red and white eyes, and a mean streak so broad it left no room for any other streak. That goat lived to butt, and though tethered, he could get just about everywhere in the lawn. He was tethered to mow and keep the woods' undergrowth back, not to be restrained from chasing down small or medium-sized children and whatever other prey he fixed on. He was a self-appointed guard goat. Alone, I would often just stand by the back door and watch him watch me.

Sometimes when I was taken to Florence's, there would be

two older kids visiting there, a brother and sister, and they managed to make a game not only of the goat but of me and the goat or, if he was with me, my real first cousin Tim and me and the goat. They would chase us into the range of the goat and we would have to use our wits to avoid his horns. The yard was on one side blocked in by a low plane of sticky marsh with sharp marsh grass that could poke through the fabric of pants and the skin of knees and palms. The other side of the yard ran along a dense hedge of closely pack saplings, snarled with honeysuckle vines and blackberry brambles, with poison ivy and oak. At the back, the full length of the yard, all within range of the goat, was a five-foot drop and the beach. When I was small and at Aunt Florence's, that bank seemed a cliff, with cement footholds and a flimsy iron railing leading to a narrow beach. Older, I realized that that cliff was less tall than my father, who then stood six-foot-two. But even knowing this, in my memory as I have gotten older, I find I have filed that bank in memory as a tall vertical cliff.

Aunt Florence's place was dangerous — there was the goat, there were sometimes the older kids, and there was no escape, just the road at the front and the sharp bank down to the beach and the Magothy at the back. But the visit I remember most sharply and most darkly is this one.

Every time my grandmother and I went off driving alone, I was usually very quiet, but not comfortable with the silence. I strained against it, feeling we should be making conversation. I ran topics through my head like flash cards and often said something silly, trying to break the tension I felt. I didn't feel this tension when we picked berries or weeded. Berries and weeds became our topics, and our hands were busy, but when it was just the two of us, alone, driving, I found the silence loud and embarrassing. So I asked questions, and I learned.

The Ritchie Highway is divided by a grass median strip; our lane this particular day the one headed east. At one point in our drive, we pass a spot on the far side of the west lane, a cozy pull-off into what is just acres and acres of woods. The pull-off is probably long and deep enough for three cars to parallel park. The ground there is dirt. Sometimes there are people standing there, just one or two. Never a crowd. During this one trip to Aunt Florence's, I see there is one person standing in that spot, a woman with deep caramel skin, very dressed up, as if for church. I see her high heels and her hat with its veil. I have wondered about this pull-off for a long time. It looks inviting, someplace I would like to stop and explore. Every time I have ridden towards Annapolis and back, I have watched for and contemplated this pull-off. This day, on our way to Florence's, I finally ask about it. I ask my grandmother, "Why is that colored lady standing over there?" My grandmother's answer has the snap of a mouse trap, the flick of the end of a whip.

"Never call a colored woman a lady." She said each word solidly, evenly. I don't ask why. But in that moment I hate the word *lady*. I have hated the word ever since. I was probably nine or ten, but even then, it seemed wrong that while my sisters and I were always supposed to "act like ladies," others were not allowed to *be* ladies. I played that memory over in my head many times until I understood and could name where my grandmother was coming from. After that, I replayed it because I wanted to remember what I understood and the feeling that I had, way before understanding, of being washed over by a darkness and chill that had settled down hard and sudden on that vivid, hot summer afternoon.

Two   Naming. What's in a name? Everything. *Would* a rose by any other name smell as sweet? I don't think so. Imagine a rose now named kudzu or vetch — would Beauty's father have risked his life and her for single flower of vetch? Would the Beast have bothered with thieves after kudzu? Kudzu fills the air with a scent of grapes — not unlike Koolaid grapes. Vetch, itself, is scented not unlike a tea rose. In the prime of sultry summer, the air along interstates in Pennsylvania grows thick with the perfume of vetch.

Of course, one might argue that kudzu and vetch vine and are thus unsuitable for vases and nosegays and boutonnieres. Roses are versatile, bushes with ready bouquets, angular climbers for hiding architectural flaws and draping to create fragrant shade. Roses can be statuesque and individually outstanding. The history of Crowned Vetch can be traced to the labs at Penn State University and the history of Kudzu to China, a legume vine whose roots provide starch and whose vine provides fiber. Roses fill the poetry of the most ancient Persia and ramble through legends and songs of the British Isles.

There's without doubt something to a name. One would not necessarily hope for a dozen long-stemmed vetches to mark an anniversary, a single kudzu for one's bud vase. "The Yellow Vetch of Texas" might scan the same tune, but "Sweet Kudzu of Avondale" or "My Wild Irish Loosestrife" would lose their melodies.

Or take a kitten, perhaps a better example because roses are so fixed, so uninteractive. Kittens happen to us and us to them. Name that kitten Slugger. Take that same kitten and name him Harrison. Take that same kitten again and let the neighbor child name him Tiny Kitty. Could he possibly grow up to be the same cat with those different names? I don't think so. Slugger will get roughed up and thus become rough. Harrison will be treated with more dignity and become aloof. Tiny Kitty will become an oddity, named by a child who even as she grows up sees the absurdity in having a fifteen-pound cat named Tiny Kitty. So he'll be shortened to TK — not his real name, not the name he's learned — and perhaps his features will blur. His stripes will widen and leach into his ginger fur until he can sleep in a tight curl and an observer cannot tell where he begins and ends. Perhaps his identity will blur.

Take me. I was named Elizabeth Scott Hodges, a good Anglo Saxon Southern name, not Elizabeth Susannah or Elizabeth Sarah. Elizabeth itself was too long and got snipped to Betsy, one of around thirty possible cuttings. By the time I got "Betsy," others had already done things to the name. "Sweet Betsy of Pike" had taken up with Ike and a Red Shanghai Rooster and an Ol' Yeller Dog. Sweet Betsy had bare feet, pig tails, buck teeth, and wore the same dress in every song book I saw in grade school. She was a hick, a bumpkin, while "Old Betsy" was a gun, Davey Crockett's, yes, but a rifle nonetheless. When I was four, one toy company, one I will forever boycott, introduced Betsy Wetsy. Let me be gross here. Because of that doll, a doll which did nothing but get filled up with water at the top end and then, when squeezed hard, emptied of water at the other — because of *that* doll, Betsys my age went through grade school to the rhythm of "Betsy Wetsy, two by four// Couldn't get through the bathroom door//So she did it on the floor//Licked it up and did some more."

Betsys, I think, at least those of the Betsy Wetsy era, had no option but to become writers, poets at least of doggerel with which to arm themselves in response. Language was the only civilized avenue of defense. There are many writers who call themselves Elizabeth. I wonder how many have a Betsy inside them.

But Betsy is also a name for Carolina Allspice, Sweet Betsy, the plant I grew up hearing called a Shrub. But I did not learn about this Sweet Betsy until after I had, in an effort to transform myself into an Elizabeth, inadvertently became a Liz. Lizard. Lizard Breath. Lizzy. What people don't realize, I think, is that just as Slugger and Harrison, or "Hey Babe" and "Excuse me Ma'am," create different cats or women, so do Betsy, Elizabeth, Liz and Lizard create different versions of the same person.

Had I been a boy, I would have been Charles Addison Cook Hodges. CASH. Perhaps I'd have been rich. As it is, I'm ESH. Sort of amorphous. Sort of versatile, like a suffix. That's not a bad thing, necessarily.

As I've gotten older, I have met an increasing number of women who call themselves Betsy in all arenas. I meet more all the time, grown women who never tried to shed the Betsy like I did. Grown women, with real professional careers and serious ambitions, aspirations, who have a solid Betsy identification. I am amazed by them. Betsy is what I call myself most of the time, what my family and a few pre-Liz friends call me, but Betsy is not my public face. Or perhaps it is, and I just don't know it, thinking that I meet the world with that face goes by the name of Elizabeth or Liz.

All Betsys have at least one thing in common for sure: throughout their lives, people, children and adults, poets and non-poets alike, have spelt Betsy wrong — Besty or Bestey or even Bestie. Most of my nieces and nephews, youngest to oldest, still do address me in writing this way. Many Betsys, too, have (some much to their embarrassment) been misunderstood when they introduced themselves and are heard to say Bitsy. Like Itsy Bitsy. I remember going for my first real riding lesson the spring I was twelve and the teacher, a teen five years my senior, misunderstood what I'd called myself and kept calling out loudly, from the center of the riding ring, "Bitsy, there's daylight between your legs. Bitsy, get rid of the daylight." So distracted was I by her calling me Bitsy when I was not bitsy, when I was taller than everybody, boy or girl, in my class, when I was developing breasts and hips and feeling always clumsy in action and spirit — so distracted was I that I stiffened and my reddened ears ceased to filter. I could learn nothing from her that day and know I seemed to her the most unlikely of students. I sat the horse unsteadily, even at a walk, with all the grace of a simple, powerless clothespin slotted over too thin of a line.

As a Betsy who shed the name for whatever I could get, embracing whatever I got, I wonder sometimes if someday I will return to being a Betsy. I wonder how that might feel. Betsy is a shadow figure, yet a force within me, strong. Sometimes I think that if I returned to Betsy I could be, would be, free.

Three   When we moved to Pennsylvania, I had a list of names I wanted erased from our memories. This is not to say that these names were ever on the tongues of my parents, my sister, or me, but they were names that were part of the symphony of the language I grew up hearing. By fourteen, I had seen enough shadows cross my parents' faces when this or that uncensorable relative said "nigger" or "boy." Such names are drenched in shame as much as viciousness. Growing up, I soaked up that shame as my own, a shame I never heard in curses. Curses are thrown, like stones, plates, rotten tomatoes, objects that miss or glance off their targets. The names we moved away from were spears which, once aimed and cast, pinned their targets in place like butterflies on a board, illuminated and labelled.

I do not like to write these names, but I have needed to write about them. They are part of the elements of my history and when I write that history, these names echo in my ears still, swimming there at times when I am thinking of then — thinking of the river, the grandparents, the relatives, the other people. Such thinking has never been neutral. These people are my ghosts, and it is in part their language that haunts me. The river was and is silent. It still glistens and beckons. I do not even have to close my eyes to see it. The voices I associate with it, calling from along its beaches and cliffs sometimes crowd in and swell and mute the river's silence. I cannot hold my hands over my ears and ignore those voices. And somewhere in that juncture of silence and voice, water overlaps sand and rock, and guilt nestles in and drops tentacles like roots. It may not be my guilt, but I always felt it as though it were. I start to say that the crimes that created it were embedded not so often in action as in language. But then I know that to name is the major action of language.

Baptism is an act of naming and consecrating. People baptize others when they give each other names that stick and endure.

Blood and Blue Willow

My adults were enamored with the past, not with who *we* were as individuals, but with *who* we were according to who our ancestors were, the glorious sum of *us*. It had something to do with the color and thickness of our blood, a notion that took me a bit to catch on to, to get metaphorically. I knew my blood was thick because cuts didn't bleed long. My blood clotted fast and still does. A friend of mine, Todd, always bled the same color as me but he didn't clot as fast. When we poked our fingers with a small, sharp auger to, yes, become blood brothers, he bled a lot longer than me though his poke was no deeper. I thought I noticed some color difference between when he bled from his nose as opposed to a cut, but I expected my blood would differ similarly had I been one of those nosebleed kids. I remarked on all this finally to my cousin, and he set me straight real fast, took me down the hall between my grandparents' bedrooms and instructed me about the black-framed coats of arms hanging there. I'd never noticed them particularly, probably just putting them in the same visual category as oriental rugs — designs that had color and sometimes rhythm, but no special visual meaning. Like dress material. My cousin, disgusted, told me, and not for the first time, that I really had to have been adopted. I was so dumb. I couldn't feel my own blood. After he had gone home, and many times after that lecture, I went back to study those coats of arms. For a while, I became obsessed with trying to understand them. "Latin" my grandfather told me when I asked about the elements I recognized as writing, but he didn't stop to translate. I don't know if he even could.

Studying those coats always got me feeling funny, bad funny, sick. Even now, as I write this memory down, I feel a tightening pressure just below my voice box. But why? And where did those coats go after my grandfather died? Probably to his oldest son since he'd disowned the younger son, youngest of three children with my mother in the middle, purportedly for marrying a Catholic and adopting two children. At least that's what I've always understood. That younger son, my favorite uncle on my mother's side, moved half a country away and I never saw him again until my grandmother's funeral years later. Soon after, when my grandfather went to live with Uncle Carver and Aunt Edith, he must have taken the coats with him, and I guess when Carver died, they passed to my only male cousin on that side of the family. Boys always counted first, and my cousin, the one who clued me in about the coats in the first place, would have wanted them. I wonder if they hang on his wall? I hope, if they do, that he sees them as historical artifacts, not icons. I would like to see them again if only for their place in my personal history — their colors and shapes, their words, the names of family strands I know little about. When I was a kid, though, they eventually led me into a sort of pugnacious positioning of myself against my ancestors, immediate and distant. Understanding how my adults — and my own generation of relatives — felt about those coats filled me up with resistance, rather like I felt towards the Jesus miracles, actually. I wanted to reason them through, solve their puzzle, expose them to bright light. Loaves and fishes to feed too many? Slice the bread thin and stretch the fish by making fish salad sandwiches. I had been suspicious from an early age, perhaps after Captain Kangaroo convinced me to plant a precious nickel in a flower pot in an effort to grow a money tree.

On Sundays, regardless which side of the family we ate Sunday supper with, it seemed like the all discussions led to the past, the far past, the glories, the losses.

Just as I was neither intrigued nor awed by the coats on the wall in my grandfather's study or those in my father's mother's dining room, I was not spellbound by genealogies and detailed histories of who came when and lived where and did what and married whom and died how at how old in what way. There are many family stories I can tell, but they would not be the stories I was told on Sundays to make me proud of who I was, to make me behave like a lady.

At the time I got my lesson about the coats, I was round-faced with straight fly away hair, what my cohorts called dirty blond or dishwater blond. I had two cowlicks, one in front and one on the top of my head. I had a ski jump nose and round brown eyes, ever ruddy cheeks in a round face. When I looked at myself in the mirror, I knew for sure that I would look that way all my life. I knew that no miraculous spurt of growth would thin me upwards and no sudden mystery of womanhood would turn my plain round features to elegance and beauty. Not even make-up would help. So I looked at my face and wondered, "Where are the Welsh warriors and French knights? Where are the Irish devils and the British lords?" They were not in my face or in my blood anywhere as far as I could tell.

Nor did the knowledge of *them* have much to do with what made me a little proud to be me, proud of climbing trees faster and higher than my male cousins, of getting lots of As in school, of swimming under water so long people started wondering if I'd drowned, of catching crabs alone in the canoe, of beating up the two boys up the road. Those things had nothing to do with crusty old documentations of ancestors, with stories of who got here how early and owned what and lost what — *wonderful* whats that would have come to us, should have come to us, had *this* or *that* not happened. Failures always had external explanations — the War Between the States, for example. When I wondered why, with these special ancestors, we were so poor that I could not have my own horse or go to Disneyland, the answer always lay in the tricks of kismet or human ignorance. My ancestors were men who were "ahead of their time" and built wonderful futuristic motors, docks, buildings, ships — whatever — that received only public scorn because the public was ignorant. So "fortunes were lost." And while now I can see that such ignorance and fear of the innovative do exist as a powerful force, it struck me odd then that so much glory could be so lost that nary a trace was left. And if they did indeed lose everything, then why should we have admired them so or have lodged our own senses of worth in their precedence? I mean, what precedent did *that* set? As far as I could see, no one in our family on either side of my family owned much, except for one branch on my mother's side, yet the older people spoke as if it were just yesterday that some ancestor was invited back to England to take up a lordship and a manor. And he refused. And why? Because he was, though of royal blood, a true patriot.

And crazy as a rabid raccoon as far as I was concerned. Nutso. Absolutely unbelievable. My mother and I shook our heads at his idiocy each time the story got told. In secret, she had almost as little use in her own way for these ancestors as I did, and I had no use for them at all.

Except for this — I soared at the idea of things lost or misplaced. Things that might be found again and might just save us from the "poverty" of Dad in school at nights, piano lessons for me, art lessons for my older sister, school clothes and shoes for three kids. Things that would get me that horse.

Several books excited my imagination. There was one about a poor, poor family somewhere in Pennsylvania or Ohio or Iowa. They were so poor that they made the oldest two girls leave school to get jobs to help at home with money and chores. The oldest, Caroline, didn't mind. She was beautiful, not terribly into school, and was ready to get on with finding a good husband, which would be no small challenge from her impoverished position in the world. The next oldest, Margaret, was heartbroken. She had been assured by her beloved teacher, Miss Hester, that she would indeed be able to get a teaching certificate and become a teacher too. But her father didn't care. He thought girls should marry and take care of husbands and homes and have lots of children. Girls should marry good men who would be like sons and enhance the future by coming from better families. Her father didn't want any of his girls "growing up old maids." Teachers were always old maids, it seemed. But the next oldest, Amanda (there were nine kids, the youngest the only boy), well, Amanda was my age and she was still in school, but knew her time to leave would come too soon. She worried about that and worried about Margaret who was very brave, but tended to cry silently when no one was looking.

Amanda was a good girl who did her share of chores, but she was also a tomboy and an explorer. One day, out in the hilly woods where she was stealthily sneaking up on the sound of rustling leaves behind some dense bushes, she moved slowly enough that she saw a dark crevice she'd never noticed in the stony, lichen-coated face of a granite cliff she passed all the time on her way to school. An immense and ancient tree had fallen during a storm the night before and stripped down the overgrowth of mountain laurel and wild rhododendron that had long hidden the gap. Of course, in this story Amanda moves in for a closer look. The crevice is pitch black, of course, and of course she has no light and yet and yet — and yet she feels a draft coming out and dares to squeeze into the crevice enough to sense a good-sized space, to imagine a cave within. She scurries home, tells no one. She squirrels away candle wax in an old cracked drinking mug until she has enough to support a purloined wick. Then she goes back to explore that cave.

One thing leads to another and Amanda finds these barrels (the crevice was once a wider opening) packed carefully with lovely linens, carefully wrapped in paper against dirt and yellowing. And nestled in these linen-stuffed barrels is fine bone porcelain china, very old, but in pristine condition, with the famous Blue Willow design. There are enough place settings to serve sixteen people at a large table. There is even a miniature set for a child.

Of course these dishes are terribly valuable and, of course, once Amanda tells of her find, the china causes much turmoil for her poor family members who want to be good, honest people, but want and need to be richer. In the end, they find an address on one of the barrels and through it trace the heir to these dishes, a wealthy young man in San Francisco. He is so excited by Amanda's find that he hurries east to see these wonderful plates which had belonged to his great-great-grandmother, an early pioneer. The dishes and some other family treasures had had to be left behind when a wagon horse's death forced the travelers to sacrifice their second wagon. The china had been hidden, according to a family legend, in a cave which no one had ever been able to find again. These precious plates had become a legend.

So filled with joy is he by the dishes that he rescues Amanda's family from its poverty with a generous reward, falls head over heels in love with Caroline, returns Margaret not only to school, but to a school in San Francisco, so she can be near Caroline. And this wonderful young man supports the private education of the other children while they continue to reside with their parents, now farming, with adequate help, a fine sheep farm. Or was it hogs?

Needless to say, the farm thrived and expanded and all lived happily ever after — because of lost dishes found and, with integrity and no expectations, returned.

It did not cross my mind to wonder just how much money such dishes might really have been worth. I imagined Blue

Willow very differently from the design I eventually came to know and, without even liking, purchased a piece of here and there at garage sales and flea markets, even after I was well into adulthood. Just in case. I asked my father if his family had ever had Blue Willow plates. He groaned. *Yes.* He ate off them all his life and he hated them. But they were valuable, I informed him. *They are gone*, he responded. So I began what would become a multi-yeared and redundant search of his mother's attic and basement, looking for valuable lost things or valuable undiscovered natural resources. In numerous forays I searched and pried and dug and dismantled. I would give up and then return to the search when something inspired me to search a little differently. In the warren of small attic rooms I found old *New Yorkers* with cartoons I could not fathom. I found old toys — metal horses pulling ice wagons and fire wagons — old clothes and commemorative plates, Tippecanoe and Tyler too. I searched through leather and wood trunks for old papers and letters. Maps with an X. I found no plates other than red glass plates, pretty but not Blue Willow. In the basement I pushed past the old furniture and tools and dug in the dirt of the half basement. Even now, my own half basement makes me pause and wonder. Recently, when my goddaughter visited, she asked if I had found any secret panels or doors yet. Her mother laughed. But *yet. Yet.* There is, after all, always the hope of the find.

More often I had the opportunity to steal into my mother's mother's attic since she lived next door. I was a mouse of silence. The attic was taboo. But I left no trunk or old wooden chest drawer unopened or unoverturned. I searched for envelopes taped underneath or behind drawers. At one point I found a single piece of Confederate money in an old filled ledger, the ink so faded to rust that I could not tell what the writing meant. But though worthless, this piece of defunct money shifted my gaze from china plates. Money is, after all, easier to hide than china.

I began again, checking through envelopes and books, even the books high up on shelves in both my house and my grandparents'. I pried up any loose board and sifted through the cottony insulation where floor ended and only rafters supported my feet. Looking for signs of slits stitched, I studied every inch of the mattress on the old brass double bed and the cushions on the retired Morris chair. For three years at least, I lived for attics and crawl spaces and basements, looking for any hiding place, tapping for any sign of hollow places behind walls.

And just about the time I'd decided to give up my search for ancestors' contributions to my worth, fate would have me read some new books about finding. Little Eddie found the clay porcelain was made of. Nancy Drew found endlessly. In *Ding Dong Dell* a cat chased by boys lands on a hidden, rotten board covering an old well. The board gives way, the cat falls straight down and lands, with all four sets of claws clenched, on a cushiony brown paper package lying dry at the bottom of the well. The daughter of this also poor family gets her dear older brother to lower her down, a rope around her slender, twelve-year-old waist, till she can grab the cat, hold it against her breast, and be pulled back up. The cat is fine, but scared, so scared that it cannot retract its claws from the brown paper package until both he and it are out of the well and on firm ground. The package is tied with string. Once out of the well, coddled and crooned to, the cat recovers its nerve and lets the bundle go and it breaks open to reveal bundled paper money, big bills. The poor family has made easy money from the claws of a cat, now a member of the family. But like Amanda's family, this one is also honest. They report their find to an also honest sheriff who runs an ad that reads something like, "Money Found! Name the correct amount and claim what's yours!" So the family waits and waits and waits till the claim period is near done, and of course, the day before waiting ends and the money is theirs, a narrow serious man with brown moustache and brown hair in a brown suit comes and names the right amount. But it turns out that he and a now-dead comrade had robbed a bank and he has fallen into a trap set by that bank and the sheriff. The bank robber is charged with the murder of his partner as well as the robbery, and the bank comes across with a bountiful reward which solves the poor family's financial woes.

My searching expanded to include scouring the land around me for abandoned wells and caves, for hollow trees, for signs of ground dug up and carefully replaced. Even now, when I go into my own attic, I can't help but wonder what's under the insulation or if there is any hidden hole beneath the boards. And there have had two finds, a green glass jar with top that my mother found when cleaning out the canned goods room in the basement and a brass fireplace shovel I found in an actual hollow beneath the attic floor. I had been looking for my cat.

In my back yard there is a cement block. Carved into it are the initials C.V.T. For the first two years I lived here, knowing that backyard graves were common in the south, I assumed it to be a grave marker and hoped whoever or whatever was buried there did not mind me using the marker to elevate my cookout grill. One of my colleagues, a somewhat nervous woman, would not eat dinner with me if she knew I was cooking on the grill on top of what she was sure, and what I'd made no effort to convince her otherwise of, was a grave. But as I learned the history of my house, I began to wonder. Perhaps? No. Could that stone be a marker for something else, some buried treasure rather than a grave marker. Illegal to dig up. But C.V.T., what did that *mean*?

In 1993, on a walk in the Fan District of Richmond, I found another such marker, also marked C.V.T. I did not need my cousin this time to show me the light or a Latin book to help me in translation. Central Virginia Transportation or Transit. It was a trolley block. But.

Even now, in fact, even perhaps more now that I know the block is not marking a grave, I wonder what might be beneath it. I mean, why is it in *my* back yard? No trolley ever passed on my street, so I cannot help but wonder if there is actually something buried there. I wonder if I will one day look to find out.

My thoughts here have moved a long way from those coats of arms which made so much of my family feel, as my father puts it these days, "like something great on a stick." There's one, actually, that I would like to hang on my wall because it resonates with the resistance I have always felt, even if first instinctively, to ancestor worship. This coat of arms was one that had been stripped to nothing but a peacock's fanned tail. Why? Sort of a political strip poker kings played with their noble lessors. Each time the lessors resisted the king's edicts in some way, a part of their coat was ripped away until they ended up with nothing left to lose. I don't know what they resisted or if I would agree with them. I write for myself their history because I want there to be in that peacock's tail a tale of simple honesty of self, of resistance to imposed beliefs, resistance to any better than thou-ness, a resistance I acted out even before I could articulate what it was or why it got me up in arms.

Baptism IV
Jim Brew

I am, perhaps, five. A group of us, all family, perhaps from both sides, is walking down College Avenue from the school parking lot towards Main Street of Ellicott City, Maryland. We are walking down the narrow and uneven sidewalk that graces the right side of the street, a sidewalk uneven with bricks or cobbles, a sidewalk which creates a path between the street and the dark red wooden warehouse of the B & O station. We are heading to a parade, most likely a Fourth of July parade, and we are early, set on finding a place to stand and wait. On a chair up on one of the train warehouse platforms sits an elderly black man, coal black, his eyes rheumy. I remember him as ancient, though he must have been only in his early sixties. My father recognizes him at once and speaks to him with familiarity, respect and affection. The man recognizes my father and they talk a bit about their mutual past. Then my father introduces me to the man. I am young enough that such an introduction is a matter of putting me on the platform next to the man and announcing who, perhaps where, I am. The man takes my hands in one of his. His hand, I remember clearly, is huge and strong and its palm soft, velvet. The man pulls me close to study my face and tells my father how beautiful I am, how much I am surely his child and my mother's. Someone says loudly that we must go, go and find a place to stand, a place from which to watch the parade. *Why not this place?* I wonder. In fact, I might have asked that question aloud. How could I not want to stay with this old man who finds me so special? But I am plucked down from the platform and we move on, down to the main street, and find a place where it is more crowded and more white, and the women with us, not my mother, talk for quite awhile about how my parents must get me in a bathtub as soon as they get me home. I remember the words *slobber* and *drool* associated with the old man.

Words, like snapshots, I record and review, and when the time comes that I can contextualize and interpret them, I look at them harder, wishing I had been older and more able to participate in what has become a compelling memory. Years after the encounter I ask my father about this man because he has, for some reason, stayed with me for decades. My father tells me he was called Jim Brew because he would always carry his little pail to the back doors of the pubs to get his beer, but his real name was Jim Snowden, named after the Snowden family, those of the peacock, for whom his parents had worked before the Civil War and then after. My chest tightened painfully as he told me these things and tightens so again as I write this history because I know what those dates mean. My father says, "He was like family," and remembers that when he was nine and ten, Jim Brew, then in his mid-thirties, would

come to the house and trade chores for meals, weeding carefully all day in exchange for food. My father tells me too that in
the 1920s, when my great aunts, Weedie and her sister, were
teenagers, Jim, a young man in his own early twenties, would
follow along behind them as they strolled across Ellicott City
to visit their grandmother. If some man or soldier would approach them, Jim Brew would step in closer and say, "Excuse
me Sir, but I'se with these ladies." And the interloper would
back off, leaving Jim to escort the cousins on their way.

Such stories, regardless of who in my family told them,
were always related with affection, love, for individuals like Jim
Brew and the places, the relationships, they held in our history. Some often distinguished between good slave owners and
bad, as if the question of ownership was never the issue. Once
when I asked my parents about this differentiation, they asked
me, in return, if didn't I think it had perhaps been a strategy,
albeit a pathetic one, some might have adopted to lessen the
guilt they felt at their roots. And as I recount this memory now,
I find myself aware that history is very often close to us, sometimes so immediate and looming in its presence that when we
are in any way at all personally connected to events, even to
those that seem far before our birth, we cannot help but be
responsive to them, responsible for them, in how we proceed
in our living.

Dreams of
Push-Button Eyes

1962 I cannot leave well enough alone. In fact, I can rarely leave *any*thing alone. I've caught in the vise before me on my father's workbench a golf ball and slit a narrow strip out of its dimpled white skin, which I now carefully pull back with pliers. I do not want to touch the ball's emerging innards with my fingers. I have been warned that there is poison in the center, and I do not know how large the center is, how much distance there is between me, the ball's hard shell and its core. Just beneath the skin there seem to be rubber bands mashed together. I decide to skin the entire ball before digging deeper. Doing so takes almost an hour of meticulous picking and pulling, after which I remove the ball from the vise and drop it, ducking slightly behind the furnace in case the poison is a gas. The ball still bounces, but not well. With pliers I pick it up and return to the workbench. The layer beneath the shell now looks less like rubber bands than something a little more yucky, a mass of worms, perhaps the sort that writhe as they crawl in and out of a skull's snout. The pliers are too large to pick at these with any delicacy, so I head up the cellar stairs to get tweezers out of my parents' medicine cabinet. Tweezers and the sharp-pointed metal tool which has something to do with teeth.

Back in the vise, the ball gives some as I tighten down on it. The wormy mash of rubber is hard to remove. It is sticky and tight. But a thing begun must get done, and finally I do reach the core. I know it when I see it. It is like a round pill, dark brown and translucent. It seems to be filled, like a vitamin capsule. It truly looks poisonous. I release the now mangled ball, carefully ease out its deadly core, and put it in an empty match box I find on the workbench. Then I carefully clean up the mess I have made on the floor and workbench, pull the light cord, and leave the back cellar room. Night is coming. The half windows at ground level look out on a yard gone gray-green and shadowed. My mother has left with my father for Baltimore, a dinner at Jimmy Wu's New China Inn and a show at the Lyric Theatre. Between me and the door at the top of the wooden stairs is the long length of a room I must run, like a gauntlet, in the dark, passing the tall freezer, the wringer washer, shelves, places many could hide. If I get through that room there is the also dark room from which the stairs rise. I pull the final light string and race, now, through the laundry and canning room to the ping pong room and up the stairs. When I reach the top, I find that the cellar door is locked. My parents have left and the house has been taken over by a hostile spirit. My older sister, seventeen, is now in control.

I know better than to cry or yell. There is, after all, that fourth room where the half cellar begins, a deep black cave under the living room and the side porch. No one can convince me that it is uninhabited by some sort of monsters, so I sit quietly, huddled into the corner made by the wall and the door. I watch the door to the laundry and the door to the fourth room. I keep careful watch, too, through the space beneath the railing, watching for movement under the stairs and beyond the basement windows. It is pitch dark now in the cellar. No light enters from the road because there are no street lamps. Occasionally a car grinds by on the cinder and tarmac. I know tonight I will have bad dreams.

Eventually the bolt slaps back with a clack. I snap to on the move, lunging at the knob and falling up and into the kitchen. "Dinner's ready," my sister says. "Go wash your hands and face. And wash behind those ears." I don't know where she gets that ear business. Never do Mom and Dad mention the ears. But I return from the bathroom having washed behind them carefully. The usual dinner — two burgers, well done, no rolls, a mound of spinach, home-made French fries, slightly flimsy, ketchup. We eat in silence. We clean our plates, and grate-fully — too, too full — I go out into the night to feed the rab-bits in their pen. Into the large oval ivy that separates our large back yard in two, I quietly offer up a fair share of my dinner. I feel guilt, for children are always starving somewhere, but the pain of a too full stomach stretching taut as it presses my ribs further apart feels worse than guilt. I feed the rabbits and go back into the house.

My sister and I are not enemies. She is not really hostile to me, because of me, like it feels at times. She is simply eight years older than I am, and I do not interest her as much as she interests herself. She is my favorite mystery. I wish I could say the same of her. We have lived together nine years and I don't know her at all. She is bigger. She lives upstairs in our house, as I do, but always behind a closed door when I am there —

and perhaps when I am not. She is dark in hair and complexion. I am fair and pale or sunburnt. Our new sister, next door with Grandmom, has dark hair, but is pale like me. There does not seem to be as much difference between two and nine as there is between nine and seventeen. I wonder if when I am seventeen, my little sister will feel the distance I feel now as I try to figure out where to settle this evening, where to go that I will be the least of a pest.

"It's 7:30," my sister says. I ease towards the living room and the piano. "Why don't you go on up to bed."

"I *never* go to bed at 7:30," I tell her. "Do you want to play Sorry?" But even before she can say no, the phone rings, a friend, and I go upstairs and sit at my table in my room and work on my novel.

I have a lot of fears. I am afraid of the dark, but only the dark inside the house, particularly the basement. Outside in the night, on the river or the land, I feel invisible and safe. But in the house at night with all the lights off and even with everyone at home asleep, I feel terror.

I am afraid of my grandfather. His anger erupts without prediction. I have catalogued some things that will make him mad and avoid them wisely, but it seems each week I discover another three or four I add to my list. It gets long.

I am afraid of my Aunt Edith and Uncle Carver. I make them mad, too. When I stay at their house, I manage to make Aunt Edith mad every day. When Uncle Carver comes home, she tells him whatever and then he gets mad too. Two angers for the price of one error.

I am afraid of my Aunt Rebecca. When we walk up the long flagstone walk to her house we can always hear her yelling at her boys, using words like "God damn Jesus Christ Christopher" and "stinking little shit" and "you sonofabitch little shit." When we go in, it's all peace and joy. But every time we visit, she always catches me alone, on the front porch swing or the bottom back step, and tells me how good I am and how she is going to trade her boys for me. I cannot tell anyone about that and about how anxious and qualmish I feel when she says that, but my stomach truly rolls and clenches with an intent of its own.

There are not many kids near my age where I live, but of those few, there are some older boys who appear from behind bushes, around corners, from nowhere behind me, like Skeezicks or the Pipsisewah, like Mr. Lawson's black dog, like Mr. Sappington and his twelve gauge. I am afraid of them too. My nearest neighbor's son, Axel, locks me in basements, garages, play houses, attics, and tool sheds. The price of freedom varies in size. At times, I only have to eat a Milkbone — albeit for a large dog. Other times, I have to take my clothes off and let him look. And then there's Jeff who chases me with large switches and sticks. He pushes me off the end of the pier in cold weather or when the nettles are bad and then beats me to any place I might climb up. Usually, unless he is interrupted by the saving presence of an adult, I end up swimming parallel to the shore until I get to a house and see someone at home. Jeff races me along the shore until that third person appears or until I come parallel to where the shore gives way to rock jetties or cliffs.

In my novel, I am not afraid of any of those things I can't handle in my life. In fact, there's nothing I can't handle. I have a horse named Satan who is completely wild, except with me. I live in my own cabin on an island in the river. It is not that I don't like to live with my parents. They live right on the mainland and we can wave at each other from our back doors and see each other daily. But in my cottage I am alone, Satan whickering as he grazes at night, occasionally putting his head in my bedroom window. What is darkness when I am surrounded by water and protected by a wild horse who values my life above all else?

Each morning we, Satan and I, swim ashore. I change into school clothes at my parents', eat breakfast, and gallop off to school, carefully crossing roads, rearing once before I dismount and hitch my steed to the bike rack outside my classroom's window, taking his bridle off so he can graze on a long rope while I study. At lunch, I lead younger kids around the playground on his back. In my novel, as in real life, I am a great student. In my novel, as in my life, I am also not easy with my teachers. They seem to mistrust me automatically. I can't say quite how I know this, but I do. I think it is the same problem I have with my Aunt Edith and Uncle Carver, with my Grandmother next door, with the mothers of the only two girls who live near enough to play with. I am often nervous and find it hard to look people in the eye. But in my novel it is me and my horse everywhere, and together we do great deeds which go happily unacknowledged. We scoop children off the tracks just before the train. We save children who are drowning off our island. We tow broken boats ashore in the night and then gallop off unidentified. We kill poisonous snakes just before they strike infants in their playpens or sleeping elders in rocking chairs looking out at the river. We race through weather no car can traverse and get doctors for women in labor, children with concussions, food poisoning, or appen-dicitis, men who have fallen off roofs or overturned their trac-tors. And no one knows who we are and thus no one says thank you and we don't expect it. We don't need thank yous. But this is in my novel.

In real life, there is no island off the shore from my par-ents' house. There is no horse, only a heavy, old, hand-me-down, boy's bike I ride to school and lean in the bike rack outside my classroom. There is saving to be done, but I am not the one to do it, if it gets done at all. Take for instance the day the sirens were so loud so long that I knew they'd taken the single road out to the peninsula I lived on. When I heard the sirens I left school. Just left. I raced home. I knew. Sometimes you just know. And it was my youngest neighbor, Billy, three, drowned, fallen off the end of a pier where he had no business being, alone with his five-year-old brother. And if I had been there, I could have saved him so easily. But I wasn't there and in the end, Billy lay soaking the fabric of his living room sofa, pale and caving in, still in his boots and yellow slicker, his mother screaming and crying and wailing and then, seemingly calming herself by saying over and over, "It was God's will. It was God's will. We have to trust that it was God's will." My mother stands for a long time silent, her hand on the mother's arm, stroking. There are fireman dripping. There are police. And then there is Billy's father, ashen, his face streaked with tears. He shoves past his wife and flings himself down at the sofa, pulling what was his son into his arms. Embracing him. Burying his face in his son's neck. His shoulders heave. His wife sobs on, about God's will, about God's will. With her left hand, my mother grips my shoulder and guides me from this scene. As we pass behind the sofa there is the brother, frozen, still in his yellow slicker. No one is crying over him. With her right hand my mother grips his shoulder and pulls him after us, saying to everyone, no one, "I am taking Peter up to our house for a while." No one responds, and she leads us from the house, across the yard and up the road. In our kitchen she makes hot tea and cools it with sugar and milk, and she feeds Peter pound cake with her apple jelly.

Eventually, his father comes and takes him away. After that, the day fades into evening and the evening is quiet. Dinner early. Bed early. Later that night I hear her crying as she talks with my father. I hear her anger, held tight as long as she could, now an endless stream. "No *God* did that. I wanted to shake her, shake her hard. No God. Two young children, so young, go off alone to walk in the rain. Of *course* they went down to the river. Where did she *think* they would go? That little boy. I have never seen a dead child. Drowning, I live in fear of it every day." Into the night I listen to her outbursts fade to murmurs and then, before I can drift off, rise again in volume. And through the night, with my father, my mother breaks and cries for that drowned Billy and for five-year-old Peter who watched him drown, who was the only witness, and who would always be implicated in his brother's drowning because kids push kids off piers more often than not. That's what piers are for in part, after all. Upstairs I lie awake and restless. I am sure that I could have saved him had I just *been* there. I know this. Through that night I write a script of my saving Billy, a script I will often replay and refine in my mind for years to come. Like a classic film, I can call it up even now.

I write many such scripts. In them, I am always in the right place at the right time. My judgment is quick and accurate and sure. I save. I risk myself to do so. I tell my older sister that I will grow up to be a doctor who makes it so no one ever has to die again. She tells me that death is inevitable and that I'd better think of another job. But I don't believe her, not then. And I continue with my scripts in which I am always where the need is, scripts in which I thwart villains and right wrongs before they occur. But in real life, there comes the day of Audrey and the spinaround. There was so much saving that needed to be done, could have been done, could have been done by me and so many others but was not.

1964   Hang on for life. My memory comes in flashes of visuals and touch and smell. I remember that I always hung on for my life. Tall and round objects got two-dimensional and squat as we spun. I closed my eyes to slits and color gave way to streaks of gray black white. Solid form gave way to lines horizontal. I hung on for my life on one of the bars which divided the playground spinaround in four quadrants. Once each quadrant sported its own color — red, blue, green, or orange. The bars once were like chrome, shining silver. Now the entire playground toy was the color of rust and the bars scraped soft palms.

Eyes slit, hair whipping my face, I no longer could see Audrey, my fellow passenger, as she hung onto the next bar over. We both had started side-by-side at the center, but were dragged outward out by a force I will later learn is called centrifugal. Running in turns as in relays, spinning us faster and faster, were the cool girls — Susan Jane, Mary Elizabeth, Maryanne and Jennifer Jean. Two of them ran us round for a time while the other two waited to spell them, taking turns, not getting too winded. They clocked us to see how long we would take to cry out. And we could not cry out, not because they would laugh, but because they would never play with us again after school. After a while, we were ready to cry out, to give up our social lives, but by then we could not cry out simply because we could not breathe.

Usually they tired of us and stopped the spinning, most often with a sudden jerk, but sometimes they just let go and just hung around waiting to see us crawl and fall off the old spin-around, flakes from its rusting paint on our hands and knees, staggering when we tried to stand and walk away. When they stopped it suddenly, it would sometimes throw us off onto the dusty playground or to our knees, grinding them into the sharp rust. My knees were permanently skinned, my hands permanently scuffed from this game. So why did I keep playing noon after noon? Because if I could just hold on, I thought, they would be my girlfriends. And if they were, the dangers of my loner life — Jeff with his long switches and Axel with his setting of traps — would fade with time. I knew it.

But Audrey was a problem. She did not do school well. She was slow to speak and almost always gawky, a tall stick figure with a round freckled face and round blue eyes always opened wide, too wide, under too short flyaway auburn bangs. She was always dressed in the same dress, just in three different materials, all polka dots — white on blue, white on lavender, yellow on olive green. She always stood timidly waiting for someone to do something to her, to bite hit yell sneer. She always stood ready to cry. So I took her on as, well, not exactly as a friend at first, but as I took on to protect the ugly naked-necked hen that the regular hens at Aunt Edith's pick on or the runt rabbit that the mother ignores and the siblings lie on. I could not stand the sadness in her face, nor could I understand it. Soon though, we did become friends, at least at school. Years after Audrey disappeared from school, I would see polka dots and flash on her and wonder where she went, if anywhere, and why she had always run so scared. Why *was* she always so scared? But by then, years later I would wonder about my own fears as well. Why was *I* always so scared? At this time of childhood, I was torn between wanting to be included by these cool girls with their penny loafers and curled hair and madras purses and wanting to protect Audrey who went with me anywhere she could and sometimes places she should not have.

When the cool girls would stop the spinaround, I would pretend not to be dizzy, standing up quickly, but carefully. Audrey would always sit on the ground stunned, silently crying, gray with schoolyard dust, her dirtied polka dots merging with their lavender, blue or olive green backgrounds. Her sash undone. My stomach would heave and I prayed for the bell to ring before we would be coaxed back onto the spinaround again. After the bell, I would pray all afternoon that one of the girls would invite me to her house after school. Rarely did such an invitation come, and if it did, there would be some plan, some test, some trap that I always fell unsuspectingly into.

But we all have lessons we are too hopeful to learn. I would take my time leaving the school and pulling my bike from the bike rack. I would take my time walking it slowly toward the safety crossing, following the four as they murmured and bumped hips and shouted laughs and glanced back at me with we-have-a-secret eyes. I followed till they turned off towards the new houses all built so close together where fields and woods had spread out one year before. Only then would I climb onto my new blue bike, a bike I had bought myself out of money saved from allowances and made from growing muskmelons and selling crabs to the Benfield Bar and Grill. I would pedal the mile and a half home out the increasingly quiet road to the peninsula on which I lived.

There were hazards along the way. Axel and his brother Piggy, Jeff of the willow whips, Mr. Lawson's black dog. More houses popped up every year. Even though they took away the woods, I enjoyed the building of the houses, playing in basements, then pretending the skeletons of rooms were finished and mine, but more and more the houses sprouted in the patches of woods and the fields that had long separated the older homes. And the people who were buying these new houses were different, not fun. "Westinghouse people" my grandmother called them. My grandfather predicted that soon the east coast would be continuous city from Boston to DC. He predicted too that our home would disappear. "Your house won't be here by the time you're my age, Bets."

The spin-around game went on for almost three months before the old playground ride was removed, just before May Day when each grade level was to perform for our parents the square dances we had been practicing during winter months in the cafeteria slash gym slash auditorium and as the weather warmed on the blacktopped part of the playground. Audrey excelled in these dances. Her stick arms and legs became all fluid and grace; her dutchboy cut hair glinted red in the sun and danced in time and fell neatly into place, unlike when we were spun till ill or nearly ill and her hair would become clotted by sweat mixing with dust.

That day just before May Day, like every day at recess for three months preceding, Audrey and I were again the center of cool. Silently we were spun and spun faster and faster till the solid world receded into colorless shadows and black lines. I closed my eyes and watched the sun flicker on the insides of my lids, red then shadow then red then shadow, and then there was a sudden jerk, a shriek of locking metal. I flew like a cannon ball, hard through the air and then slammed into the dusty ground that was so hard from no rain that it was as unyielding as cement. I had no air in my body and darkness came and went. I could not feel my body with any coherence, and I lay there hearing the shrill, even-pitched scream of my largest rabbit when its torso got caught during an attempted escape under the buried prongs of wire fencing. Shrill and endless, inspiring of terror, paralysis. How I freed him without killing him was an action of hands blinded by fear. I did not have the strength to lift the fence up and out of the ground. We had buried it so deep. I began screaming for help, too, panicking. Then he was suddenly free and okay. Then I was suddenly sick, I was back on the hard playground, vomiting cafeteria spaghetti and meatballs onto the dirt my cheek lay against. Playground dust coated my rancid tongue, but I could not lift my face away, so I lay in my own illness.

The screaming went on and suddenly broke into vivid full-throated screams of pain. Not my rabbit. Audrey. I did not know Audrey could make so loud a sound. No one had known. The teachers mostly panicked, some yelling for the growing crowd of children to be quiet, to line up, to go inside single file, to stay away get away stay away. I felt pinned to the ground and the ground seemed to vibrate with yelling. Yelling, yelling, for someone to call an ambulance, for someone to run for the doctor whose office was a short eighth of a mile down Benfield Road from the school. Then I heard the principal's voice above them all calling for silence, calling for the teachers to take the children inside and get themselves please get everyone under control. *Please stay in control. Please don't try to move that child. No touch. Go inside. Take the students inside.*

Audrey's screams continued, loud and rhythmic. I lay with my cheek in a puddle of red sauce and white strings, slowly feeling my chest take in air, expanding in painful jerks, slowly recognizing the existence of my toes and fingers. I moved to get up and a sixth grade teacher I would come to love when I was 11 crouched by me murmuring soothing, her hand gentle on my head. I knew I was okay, just winded and scared. I had fallen hard many times before. But she forbade me to move, except away from my own vomit.

Someone got the doctor. I watched as he moved toward us, passing through my low and narrow field of vision, where he was just pants cuffs, argyle socks and polished brown shoes under a fuzz playground of dust. I could not see Audrey, see where or how she had fallen — entangled somehow with the spinaround I learned later. The doctor's voice was angry. He kept telling people not to touch Audrey, to stay away, not to try to shift the god damned spinaround, the same spinaround on which my older sister had been injured years before. I am sure she screamed then much as Audrey screamed on this day. I think now that Audrey's back might have been injured. With my sister, it had been her knee.

Eventually, evenly paced with the rise and fall wail of an ambulance coming closer, driving right off the horseshoe driveway, up over the curb, and down the side of the school to where we waited. Its tire ripped grass from dry soil, leaving a path that would remain visible well into the summer. Then my mother was there and some man in white asked me questions about pain and made me move this and that and I was helped up, checked again, and led away to my grandmother's sea green Studebaker with its swan hood piece. My mother told me my father would come later for my bike, but in a frail moment of truce it was Jeff of the willlow whips who brought it home when school was let out. He said he had not ridden it, just pushed.

In our cool living room, darkened by maples in the front and apple trees out the side, I lay on the sofa under a throw, feverish and aching, but unbroken in body. But I felt broken with guilt. So guilty. Audrey only rode the spinaround because I did. I only rode it in hopes of making friends with girls I should not even have wanted as friends. I could hear Audrey still. Her screams would haunt me for months. No, much longer. They would become the criterion against which I measured the severity of screams. I lay on the sofa replaying the day, what I could remember of it, listening to my mother working in the kitchen. And in my mind I began to try and write a script for how I could have saved Audrey, but I could not begin to imagine how, perhaps because saving her would have taken much more than being in the right place at the right time with the right skills. Saving her would have meant not being in the wrong place at the wrong time for the wrong reasons, an intentional and wise choice to be absent rather than my thoughtless and relentless need to be present.

Somewhere about this time, in my sleep, I scripted a dream that I would, perhaps will, have for years. I am in our basement, and crawling through the windows are men who look like Dick Tracy. They have sharp features and those sharp hats low on their brow. *Fedoras?* They are dressed in charcoal gray suits and narrow ties. They are very flat, almost like cardboard cutouts, but they are deadly and human, but not quite human.

They function with sensors, picking up motion, sensing solid forms like that of a child absolutely still, holding her breath, watching from under the cellar stairs. They don't *see* me, but unless I almost become one with the freezer or a wall, they know I am there and turn, one by one, targeting me. But I know their secret, their Achilles heel. Their eyes. Their eyes are push buttons, green and glowing push buttons. The men are machines. Their sensors are almost infallible, but if I can poke each pair of eyes, poking both simultaneously Three Stooges style, the eyes push in and glow red and the men freeze in place for thirty minutes. I have thirty minutes to save my sleeping parents and sisters. But there are often five to nine of these men with push-button eyes, so the pushing of button eyes is a desperate race which I could, at anytime, fail to win. The more men there are, the more the thirty minutes is diminished before the first man will come unfrozen and resume his almost errorless search to kill. In my dream, I try to decide on best solutions. Should I poke all their eyes once and run for my family? Should I be screaming out warnings as I am turning these men off? No, loud sound enables them to move faster. I don't know how I know this, but I do. Should I try to save my grandparents too? Should I just stay in the basement and turn each one off as he comes unfrozen? No. A new rule surfaces. Each man can only be turned off three times. Another rule — each time a man is turned off he stays off for ten fewer minutes — thirty, twenty, ten, zero. Should I tie them up? Why don't I tie them up? I never tie them up and I never know why not.

In this dream, I always manage, but only just, to turn them all off and dash up the stairs to save my family. Again. Again.

And with only some few precious minutes. But that is where I awaken, where the dream always ends — in my dash to save. I have tried many times to return myself to sleep to finish the dream, to find out what happens. But I cannot, so I never really know if I do save, but I must be saving because these men continue to slip through the narrow half windows into our basement and they continue to enter my dreams.

I dream of men with glowing green push-button eyes, killers, with me the only person who can divert them. I am always there. What would happen were I not?

1996 February 14 I remember, at this same time each year, standing in blood, in 1985, and not realizing its depth until hours later when, finally home and in my own living room, I look down over a glass of straight whisky and see that my buckskin tan suede boots have been crusted with blood, turned to rust about an inch above their soles, up over my toes. It is then I lose control of my calm and at 5:42 in the morning, I find myself suffocating because I cannot get those bloody boots off. Cow hide, wet from a puddle of melted slush and blood, clings to my calves and feet as if my own skin.

Upstairs, I sit on the edge of the tub, my feet submerged to the ankles in warm water, and I slide the blade of a poultry shears gently down between the flesh of my right leg and its boot. I squeeze slowly, cutting the suede down the leg, carefully, gently, till my foot is freed. Before the other leg is cut, the water in the tub turns red — only that red that blood can color clear water. There is blood under my toe nails. Sliced boots and nylons float in the tub. I have nicked my legs in several spots — minor, but the spots ooze red.

6:50 A.M. I reassemble myself, leave the house, and drive an hour to find myself at 8:00 standing in front of twenty-seven freshmen. I meant for us to talk about bibliographies, about the complexities of documentation, about why we need to document our work and to do so carefully. Instead, I am telling them without wanting to about the drive home the evening before from downtown Philly. A birthday party? No, my birthday, but not my party. I remember leaving, urging my two companions to leave, because I was feeling urgent, knowing not knowing that something was wrong. I remember the drive toward home and feeling a terrible, hollowing fear and then seeing the surreal movement of headlights arching from the expressway above us as a car dove over the guard rail to the East River Drive and landed some decent yards, on its roof, before our vehicle. I tell these freshmen about us slowing down in disbelief and stopping ten feet from this upside down car of anonymous American make. Large. Landau roof. Maybe ten years old. Rusted nicks and dents are shadows in my headlights. The car rocking. Steaming. We reverse for twenty feet and as far to the right as possible. Then car turned off, I hear only the rushing of the Schuylkill River as it races tumbling down the step falls between where I sit and the boathouses sitting silent and dark, full of sculls.

The fallen car steams. Radiator fractured, water spouts over the hot manifold. The engine is dead. No sound but the falls rushing and a sound I realize is coming from my throat, a metallic click. One companion and I go to the trunk for whatever, a crowbar, gloves and then she and I approach the car with dread.

I tell my freshmen this in explanation of why I cannot, after all, teach our class this day. They sit frozen and silent.

Some seem angry, but I go on, relentless with a need to tell.

I tell them of approaching the car, not wanting to look. I have never been one to stop, even pause, at an accident. I get no thrill from others' tragedies. In fact I always turn my head away, not wanting to add embarrassment to injury. Accidents leave people so raw, so exposed. But I must stop, we must stop, for this accident, and I must do, we must do, something. We are the only two around. My third companion has stayed in the car and we do not blame her. So in the silence we approach the car till we see the silhouette of a man, his face pressed into the roof, head pinned between the headrest and the ceiling, neck at 90 degrees, but he is clearly alive. The window on his side is partly opened. His fingers stretch through a two-or three-inch gap between the window and the roof, grasping. Beckoning.

It was a warm night for February. I wanted to turn away, and I tell my students that. In fact, I do start to turn, partially, but then I go onward. At his window, I crouch down. My companion squats too. The hems of our skirts dip into the same bloody puddle that soaked our boots. I cannot see a way into the car. I am not sure I want to. But his hand is at my sueded toes. I am afraid to touch it, and when I do, his fingers clench mine for a second, so much stronger than I would have expected. I pry my fingers loose, get up, and with my companion, a nurse, circle the car. I am unprepared for this event, with only crowbar and gloves and a rudimentary knowledge of first aid which comes to me only in flashes of drawn pictures, almost cartoons. Tourniquets. Mouth-to-mouth.

Afraid to kick or slam at the windows for fear of rocking the car and hurting him more, we circle. The car steams. Up above on the expressway from which his car dove, a car screeches to a stop near the gaping guardrail. The expressway is so silent in the early hours of morning. A door slams. A man's voice calls down, "Anybody hurt?"

I look up. *What the hell do you think?* I want to scream. I call up, not very loud because the night is so very silent, "Yes. Very badly."

The man calls down, "Get away from the car, lady. It's gonna blow." I hear his car move off. I crouch down again by the man in the car. He has not moved. His hand lies palm upward on the black pavement in a puddle that I later realize must have been blood. I press the three middle fingers of my right hand into his palm, softly, and his palm and fingers only twitch under mine. I do not think he knows I am there. I can smell wisps of alcohol above gasoline and oil, above the burnt smell of scalding water on hot steel. I can smell the metallic rust of blood. The man is silent, but his fingers twitch. I know he is dying.

I wonder if he is coming from an evening with his girlfriend. There is a hint of aftershave and it is St. Valentine's Day after all. I cannot see his face, just its flattened silhouette, an edge of a beard and brush mustache. The river drive is not well lit. Unprepared, we have no flashlight, no flares. The skin of his palm is rough. I cannot tell if he is hispanic or black, caucasian. It does not matter, of course, but he is a dying person and I feel a need to know something about him.

I tell my freshmen that while my companion, a nurse, tried to figure out what to do I crouched there, my thighs and calves tightening to knots, until cars start arriving, slowing. People get out, but no one comes close. The steam, though much less as minutes pass, frightens them. A police car bullies through the growing spectators, flashing red and blue. Rough hands yank my companion and me back and away from the car. "Back off," the cops say. I back off slowly until I reach the roadside and stand with my companion near our car. She clutches a crowbar in her hands. We watch. One cop pops the far windows out with his crowbar. Another crawls in and yells, "This sucker is outda here."

I tell my students all this and then finally begin to cry without trying not to. Some students are crying, too. One blond guy, back left, leans back, arms crossed over his chest, legs straight out and feet spread far apart, heels dug in. He rests his chin on his shoulder and, face averted, scowls. Class is over.

I go home, call in sick for my other classes, wondering now what was wrong with me that I didn't just call in sick in the first place. Then I go to bed to dream of push-button eyes. Perhaps it is impossible to watch a person die. In the mind's eye perhaps they live briefly forever, there to die and live and die and live again. Perhaps the passing from life to death is so tenuous and fragile to be like slipping from waking into sleep into dream into consciousness.

I dream of men with push-button eyes, green, glowing, with me always there to stop them — or not.

Radio Wars,
Closed Doors,
When You're Out
I Check Your Drawers

It's 1964. In her room my sister turns her radio up high. Eighteen and a half, she shuts her door tight. Scratchy voices croon shriek yodel about love. I have peeked through the space around her door's latch and seen her dancing like some tribeswoman out of *National Geographic,* the radio urging her on from its place atop her highboy. The radio is large, over a foot at the middle from top to bottom. It is shaped like the perfect mouth of a child's notion of a cave. Mysterious with its glowing yellow tuner that makes its thick dark heavy hard plastic casing shine — it is her icon. I can imagine her in there now, facing the radio, her eyes closed lightly, her feet firm yet nimble on the oval rug our mother braided from old dresses and skirts. I can imagine her in there undulating in the tension of radio static and the tension of the time she has yet to wait before her date comes and carries her off in his car, its radio tuned to the same station, the same static, the same scratchy voices wheedling weeping wailing about love. Songs' lyrics blur.

All are war cries to my classical soul, abrasions to my ear drums. I am eleven in thirty-three days and nine hours. I am a classical pianist, seven and a half years of study stored in my long muscular fingers. For five of those years I have been working with a retired concert pianist and teacher from the Peabody Institute of Music. I am good and I see no reason for any music more contemporary than Gershwin, Rogers and Hammerstein, Lerner and Lowe, those great writers of great musicals. And of course I adore the melodious Nelson Eddy and Jeanette MacDonald. My mother loves to sing with them, and I do, too. "When I'm calling you-oo-oo-oo — oo-oo-oo." My sister sings, though I never hear her do so outside of church choir where I can always hear her voice as distinct from the 25 singers. Her voice is true and strong. She can bring a hymn to life. But outside of church her taste in music stinks.

From behind her tightly closed door a Beatles' song begins. Behind my door, also closed tight, I turn my own radio on and crank it high. Its dull plastic casing is dark and thin, etched and nicked. There's no glowing dial, but on a good day it can pull music in from Baltimore. Tonight static pricks the air in my room as in hers, but at least amid my static sing woodwinds and French horns, violins and violas, in a rich frenzy and heart-palpitating dialectic, anger ending and beginning in abrupt shifts to soft and soothing calm. Mozart's Symphony Number 40. In G Minor. Two flats. B and E. Behind her thin door, my sister's radio takes up my challenge. Some guy who can't carry a tune for a fraction of a second, whining through his nose, asks just how many roads a guy has to walk down, before he gets called him a man? *A few more than you,* I smirk. I raise

Mozart to new heights. My sister cranks her radio again. I crank and am at top volume. She is not. She cranks again and I am disarmed. She has more power. The frenzy of Mozart's first movement ends as he gives in to "I Wanna Hold Your Hand." I give in too, turn my radio off and throw my door open to glare in fury at hers. Psychic, she opens her door to give me that smile, that slightly sweet, slightly crooked curve of closed lips that always makes me feel short and misunderstood, trapped in my child body. I am nearly angry enough to yell, to lunge. But the moment is defused. Astute and always punctual, my mother calls up the stairs what is the eternal question for my sister and me, "Is anything wrong up there?" What can we do but bond and assure her? *"Oh no!" my sister responds. "Nothing!" I add. "Just playing around!" my sister adds, calling cheerfully.* I pinch my face into the worst grimace I can imagine and point it at her. *"Just seeing whose radio is louder"* is my sister's final spar. She grins and gloats. We *know* whose radio is louder. Mom retreats, knowing that *of course* something is wrong, but not what, and how could either of us explain anyway?

What would my sister say if she answered honestly? *Betsy is a brat? I hate having her in my space?* (The whole second floor of our small house truly *was* her whole space until I was eight.) *Betsy leaves the bathroom a mess? She messes with my makeup and ruins the Noxzema?* Guilty as charged. Guilty as charged. I make messes and don't see them until someone else does. I ruined her mascara, but accidentally. And it left telltale smudges and streaks that I didn't see. And the Noxzema, I *use* it. I wash my face with it. Mom buys it. I don't want blackheads and pimples to grow because my grandmother loves to go after them with bobbie pins. I have watched her corner my older cousins and check their ears and fidget around their noses. She loves their backs the best, and I know she has sharp nails. So I use the Noxzema just like it says to on its label. But last week I left the lid off and the white cream yellowed and developed a thick skin, pulling away from the side of the jar. My sister said it was done for, didn't even put the lid on it, just left it on the back of the toilet where I'd left it till it was beyond rehydrating, a shrunken hard marshmallow stuck in cobalt blue glass. Now it has become crisscrossed with fissures like the parched arid regions in the *National Geographic.*

She could tell Mom, *I don't trust Betsy to stay out of my room when I'm out?* And there is absolutely no reason she should. I have graduated from sticking to the narrow confines of that invisible trail she demarcated several years ago, running straight from her door to my office. I am now up to opening and looking into *any* box, *any* drawer, her *clo*set. I have not progressed to touching and lifting and might not. But looking and studying the artifacts of my sister has become serious work, the work of the solver of mysteries, the work of the anthropologist. Who is this young woman with the dark chocolate hair? What does she think? Want? Love? *Is she afraid of anything? It never seems so anymore. Does she know her future? Does she love this boyfriend? Does she kiss him? Does he write her love letters? Where would she keep them? The mattress.*

This is much more than nosiness. I *need* to know her and I hunt her down amongst her possessions, but I haven't found her yet. I find parts — a silver filigree friendship ring, a sand dollar from our trip to Florida.

The best part of that trip was when we drove out to Sanibel Island and across the sandbar to Captiva Island. My piano teacher, with whom I shared a passion for shells, told my parents and me about these islands. So we went to find them and there on Sanibel was a resort under construction, not necessarily open for business, but happy for visitors when they showed up. We stayed five days, a week perhaps, in a two-room cottage, for twenty-five dollars a night. The restaurant was open and the food clearly gourmet even to my neophyte palate. That's what the chef said. "You haf a ney-o-feet pal-laht, mademoiselle, but clear a good pal-laht. I will train eet some, n'est ce pas?" And he did. He did. My sister got a crush on the waiter, Ed, red hair, zits. He took us into the jungle part of the island, birding. Anhingas. Wood storks. Real ivory billed woodpeckers, not the pileated we often see in the Catoctin National Park. Ivory billed, not extinct yet after all. He took us shelling. We waded, me chest deep, feeling with our bare feet for sand dollars. He and my sister held hands under the water. I was in the way, inevitable, but invaluable. They couldn't leave our temporary home without me. So they held hands whenever they could and probably nothing more, no kissing, just static, and at times for fun I pushed against the limits of my value on the Gulf side of the island, where we'd walk to look for sharks, me following eight feet or so behind, puckering my lips and making kissy sounds. And singing their joy sweetly, quietly. "My sister has a boyfriend."

The strait between the islands and the west coast of Florida was crystal clear like an aquamarine and protected against sharks by dolphins. White pelicans sat everywhere, on each piling, on the dock, in the water. When we left, I brought back twenty-five sand dollars, several conchs, and some other shells — all priceless to me, all alive until Ed helped me commit molluskicide and store the sand dollars and shells in Clorox and water in big pickle jars in the trunk of our car. All the way back to Maryland the scent of dead mollusks grew greater and seeped around the invisible gaps between trunk and passenger compartment into the back seat. The smell was horrendous, sickening, but the shells made it home and into my collection.

I wonder if she keeps the sand dollar to remember Ed. I wonder who gave her the silver ring. I wonder and wonder but I can never put the pieces together. She is the puzzle I may never solve. I feel time getting close because she is almost an adult. She might move out too soon for me, but not for her. She knows me. She is right. When she leaves for her date tonight, I am going to explore one or two of the narrow shelves in her closet and I am going to lift her mattress to check for love letters. And if I find any, I might just read them. I am also thinking about unplugging her radio.

So what would I say if I answered my mother honestly when she asked if there was anything wrong up here? *There are too many rules up here, Mom? Why can't I read for a while before I go to bed? Reading under the covers with a flashlight is not all it's cracked up to be. Bach went blind partly because he spent his childhood nights secretly penning masterpieces by the light of the moon. Why can't I have my radio on low when I go to sleep? Why can't I turn on my light when I have a nightmare or when I simply can't sleep? Why does she always promise to "tell"?* And why don't I let her? What would have happened if she did tell? And would she ever really tell?

But most important, I would ask Mom, *Why am I only a pest? I am a pest, it's true. But I wouldn't be if I didn't have to be. Do you understand? I have to be a pest. I am too young to be a friend.*

As Mom retreats, no doubt to confer with Dad, we too retreat to our rooms and our secret identities as tormentors and tormented. She turns her radio up, just some. I leave mine off.

Through the wall between our rooms, I can hear the

Beatles again. Stupid stupid stupid music. I hate the Beatles, partly because their music does not, for me, qualify as music, but more because they drive girls, even my age girls, googah. Everybody *loves* the Beatles. Every girl in the fifth grade has picked out which Beatle she's going to marry. People go to Beatles concerts just to stand on their seats and scream so loud that they cannot even hear the music they paid to hear. So they didn't *go* to hear the music. It seems like the Beatles get paid just to come out in front of an audience to get screamed at. In some way or another, the Beatles surround me all day and all night.

But not this evening. With two of my sister's cotton balls soaked in warm water and wrung out, I shut my door and wedge myself into the right corner at the head of my bed, the furthest point in my room from the wall that separates her from me. I stuff the cotton balls into my ears and pull one of the books from beneath my pillow. I try to lose myself and my fury in the trials and tribulations of *The Middle Sister*, about a girl from the pioneer days, true, but her story is the same as mine except that she gets a chance to do something so brave that she is never just the middle sister again. She makes an apple tart for an Indian who comes into the house while her family is in town and she is supposed to be cleaning and making dinner for their return. Her fear is split between what the Indian might do and what her mother and father will do about her using the last of the stored apples to make him the pacifying tart. He eats and is peaceful when her family returns. She is a heroine. Her joy fills her chest and mine. I pull out the cotton and re-enter my world and hear silence. My sister has gone out. I tiptoe to my door, open and confirm. Her door hangs open on its black

iron pseudocolonial hinges and her light is off. I take up my
flashlight and yet another time begin my search of her room.

There are some wars between people which start in the gut
and bypass reason. My sister and I waged those wars a lot. I
knew how to get her riled. She knew just how to push me into
action against myself. Our wars, like all wars, were about terri-
tory and power. Like all wars, they began with a slightly faster
rush of blood in the veins in response perhaps to some movement almost imperceptible. Then a nudge from one side, a
pushing back from the other, a shove, a harder shove and —
escalation, elevation — the rocketing spiralling out-of-control
full-scale war, both sides doing as much as they can to give as
good as they got. Unlike most warriors my sister and I left no
gaping wounds or scars. Skirmishes were guerrilla, often silent
and devastating, quick as the strike of a snake. Retreats were
strategic and as fast as a moray drawing back into his crevice.
Only to strike again. Take the war of the closed bedroom doors,
for example. I don't know why this single conflict sticks with
me, but it does as though it occurred this morning, perhaps
because it was a true matching of wits and she won.

Our bedroom doors were knotty pine, not with knobs, but
with latches like some garden gates have: on the inside, a flat
bar is lifted and let down by a metal lever that goes through a
hole below the bar, outer door to inner door. When the door
was closed, the bar crossed the crack between door and jamb
and fell behind a metal catch on the jamb. The doors would
close, but they would not lock. Thus neither of us was secure
from interruption, invasion, and the space around the lever
encouraged spying. There was one day, though, when the issue

of locking surfaced big time. I cannot remember who started the battle. I do remember that it started as a game of sorts, fun, then less fun, then fervor, then fury.

If the lever won't move, the bar can't lift. So I stuff small wads of paper into the space around the lever. I test it. It cannot move. I go sit on my bed and watch as my sister pokes the paper out with a number four pencil. She snaps the lever up and ta-da! she has my door open. She waltzes back to her room. I try again. *If the bar is too tight, the lever won't move.*

So I fold paper until it is thick enough to force down between the bar and the door. I step back and wait, longer this time. I feel her studying the problem. I hear a grunt of satisfaction. A minute later, I watch as the thin steel blade of her painting spatula slides in and down the crack between the door and jamb and shoves my thickness of paper down and out from behind the bar. She snaps the lever up with a loud clack, opens my door, and grins her way back to her room.

If the lever won't move, the bar won't lift. So with kite string I wrap and wrap around the bar and the lever, tying them into permanent immobility. Then I sit on my bed and wait, even longer this time. I hear her door open. I feel her studying the problem. I see the white and brown ball of her eye as she peers in around the lever. I am complacent. I have got her this time. I have won. And as I settle into my warm bloodrush of glory, I see the blade of a knife slip silently through the crack between door and jamb, and she saws away at the string. This takes a while. The blade against the tangle of string grates and squeaks. The door rattles some, back and forth with each saw of the blade. As I watch, I feel the fun draining out of me and despair flooding in. Close on the tail of despair, anger edges in. The last string frays in the blade's path and she snaps the lever up and opens the door and gives me a look that seems even sad. I cannot outsmart her. She goes back to her room without a flounce. She knows the game is over. But if the lever won't move, the bar won't lift. There must be a way.

For an hour perhaps I work on creating a mess so solid that none of her ploys can dismantle it. The thickness of folded paper, tighter and longer, wadded paper, around the lever, string wrapped and pulled tight, and chewing gum hold it all together. And I wait, even longer this time. I wait. I wait. I hear no sound of her for a long time. Then I hear her radio come on and the opening and closing of bureau drawers. I sit on my bed and stare at the mess that has secured my latch and locked me in. I wait and wait more. Finally, she comes out of her room and as she passes my door on her way to the bathroom, she pauses to pull my lever out of its hole, leaving the mess of gum and paper like a sneer, the string hanging limply. *If the lever isn't there, there is nothing.*

I am embarrassed and frustrated. I am angry, too angry for the small size of my room. As I jerk stiffly towards the door to rip the mess away and get my lever back I see my right hand sweep across my bureau, knocking the surface ornaments awry. When all is still and silent, two china horses, a bay and a black, lie shattered on the floor. My heavy hand mirror lies, its glass unbroken, in the shards and dust of what had been my bank, a gold-painted pig large enough for a three-year-old to sit on. Now it is gold pieces, with pink hints of what had been flowers painted on its back. Its head lies solid but away from the body. And in the plaster dust and chunks lie silver coins, many Franklin fifty-cent pieces. I sit on the floor in silence and

disbelief. What had started as a game had ended in the wreckage of things I loved. Beyond repair. Wreckage of things loved
beyond repair. For a long time I cannot cry. I can only stare. I
can feel the wail of a child stuck in my chest. *Look what she made
me do! Mama!* But in my mind I hear the words of a non-child.
She did not make you do this. You did it yourself.

Finally I begin to assess the damage, to count the dead. I
carefully pick up the pieces of pig and limbs of horse, using my
many white cotton handkerchiefs from Aunt Edith to help me
separate the bay horse from the black and those from the gold
and pink of pig. When all that remains is dust and small
powdery white plaster chips, no longer identifiable as horse
or pig, I clean the mess off my latch and get a damp sponge
from under the bathroom sink. My lever lies on the floor outside my door. I pick it up, go in, shut the door, and set the
lever on my desk. If the lever isn't there, the bar won't lift. But
as I am wiping up dust and small pieces, my sister sticks her
lever into my door and the bar rises. She has heard the crash.
Am I all right?

I have broken two horses and my pig. I nod towards the
hankies and box. It is then scalding tears drip from my eyes.
Acid, perhaps the acid of embarrassment, they burn paths
along the contours of my face. Then cooling to chill, they drip
down into the neck of my shirt, cold drops on my chest. I am
ashamed of myself. I have broken things I loved. But no wail
accompanies the tears. They are silent. My sister squats down
and hugs me. I let her. I am not angry with her. I am angry
with everything and with myself. She stands up, fetches three
boxes from her room, and returns to carefully take my handkerchiefs of shards. I let her. And for some reason, after this
battle of the doors, I never go into her room to snoop again. I

return to the narrow trail to my office, keeping firmly to its invisible boundaries.

Over the next few weeks, my animals reappear. First the bay horse, then the black. There are cracks and white spots where chips are missing, but these only make the figures more precious. I put them on a high shelf with my other more precious objects. But when the pig returns, it is as if he never has been hurt. Missing chips have been reconstructed with plaster or spackling compound. He is freshly gold and his flowers are pink and purple and white. His eyes shine blue. They were not noticeably any particular color before. Now they are peacock blue.

I do not know for sure if I have my sister to thank for these resurrections. I would not know how to thank her if I tried, just as she would not know how to let me. A stillness grows between us. A silence. Not of anger. Just distance. I think for the first time that I recognize the distance as untraversable and accept it. In part it is age and the times, but mostly, the distance expands from what makes us who we are. Needs. Interests. Quirks. Beliefs. Creeds.

In 1966, my sister got married two days before my thirteenth birthday. I was one of her bridesmaids in yellow satin with a moss green satin sash and moss-green dyed Naturalizers — shoes with heels. In preparation, after attempts to bleach with lemon juice and sun, I was forced to learn to shave my legs for the first time. For some reason, perhaps because it was a sharp indicator that an era was ending, shaving legs was something I resisted far more than the heels I was made to practice in, walking back and forth in the living room while my grandmother coached from the sofa with the relentless precision of a drill sergeant. *Toes front, head up, back straight, toes forward, don't wobble, watch your spine.* I practiced standing up straight, shoulders pushed back against the door jam between the living and dining rooms. My posture was not that of a young lady.

On my sister's wedding day, I was inept and dead serious as I wobbled down the aisle before my older and elegant cousins. As I passed one pew, someone hissed, "Smile, Betsy." I don't think I did. The wedding proceeded as weddings do, with awkward moments and moments of grace and beauty. The reception, which I know was modest, seemed grand at the time, even though it was held in the Parish Hall, the food and punch displayed on linen-covered Sunday School tables. But it was good food. Thin slices of smoked beef tongue wrapped with water cress, livers and scallops wrapped in bacon secured with colored toothpicks, crisp vegetables and a basil chive dip, swiss cheese and rare roast beef and slices of savory sausage. Punch with strawberries and champagne. A four-man band playing music from the forties and fifties.

Eventually sensing that this was all soon coming to an end, I took a final look at the room full of people laughing, talking, feeling champagne, and I slipped outside. Inside, my sister, Kathy, five and a fine extrovert, spun in dervish windmill circles amongst the dancers, a celebration of out-flung arms. The golden streaks in her chestnut hair were lit up by the ceiling lights. Her round face tilted toward the ceiling, eyes closed, cheeks rosy, her lips closed in a perfect smile of joy. Outside, my yellow satin and moss-green, dyed Naturalizer pumps met February mud in the rainy church driveway as I made chains of cans from the caterers' trash, tying them together with crab line, the only item in my moss green Naturalizer purse with its gold link chain. Crouching, I strung the chains from the newly-weds' bumper and tucked them neatly out of sight. In the door-way to the reception, women were gathering and passing bags of rice. Purse open, I rose from the mud and went to get my share.

The Second Time
I Almost Died

I am plummeting down hill, my hands pressed so hard against either side of the horse's neck that I feel like my palms will eventually meet. His back is broad. I try to pin him between my thighs and calves, but his hide is slick, part sweat, part the greasiness of being a field horse, left out all day and night, groomed rarely, never bathed. His mane is roached, the term for a horse crew cut. To solve the problem of burdock burrs, someone has taken a clipper and shaved off the horse's mane. I am plummeting downhill, my hands becoming slick with sweat, the horse's, mine. He gives a side kick with his hind feet, a small buck, but I stay on. My immediate past is moving with mocking calm through my mind.

A few minutes ago I was standing on the ground in a lounging shed in the huge field behind my Uncle Carver's and Aunt Edith's brick house. With me in the shed, a shelter for animals which spend great portions of their lives living in fields, was my

cousin, Tim, and two teenaged strangers, a boy and a girl, sixteen at least, for they had driven up the road along the field in
an old red pickup. They had stopped because they'd seen Tim
and me poking around the shed. Tim was just nosing, but I was
there because the most beautiful horse I had ever seen was
there. I had been studying him from a distance all week.

Horses. I want. I am consumed by want. I always have been.
I love the smell of their hides. I love their soft muzzles, though
the muzzles of these horses bristled with whiskers that are
shaved off more highly groomed horses. I love their every curve
and sinew. I am and always have been besotted. I want.

Tim is immune. He really does not understand the merging of intellectual and physical, imaginative and sensual, the
absolute passion I have for horses. He says all girls are horse
crazy. He prefers a dog any day. He says he hates the smell of
horses. I respond that *I* hate the smell of dogs. I hate their
drool. I hate their subservience. I hate their canine viciousness.
Horses are rarely vicious, and never without reason. Horses are
never subservient, I tell him. They cooperate with people, but
not because they have to. The average horse has ten times the
strength of an average man, though almost all the people I
know who love horses with the intensity I feel are women,
young and old. So Tim is right, maybe, that "horse crazy" is a
girl thing, but I see nothing wrong with that.

The horse stumbles beneath me on the rocky trail. I stay on.

I had, as always, wanted. I stood in that lounging shed
wanting desperately to sit astride one of those horses. Finally I

ask the teens if I could. The girl asked if I rode. I assured her I did. In itself, this was not a lie. I do ride any time I've got a chance, often stealing into a neighbor's pasture and climbing on the back of her pony. We walk and trot and sometimes canter if the pony wants to. It took me some months of stealing rides before I could keep from bopping like an agitated clothespin off the rump of the pony when she broke into her rough trot. Up down up down up down up down she went. Bop bop, bop bop, bop bop I went, and then there I would be, usually standing, occasionally sitting on the ground watching her black rump leaving me behind. Some days she would kick up her heels as she left me behind. The day I mastered her up down up down, I felt like kicking up my own. I had learned "to post" without saddle or stirrups, I had learned about the concept of posting from a book I had bought on how to ride. I knew I had conquered something major, just as now, on this full-sized horse, I know I have done something seriously stupid.

The pony is short, like me, and narrow enough for my calves and thighs to get a purchase. She wears a red halter to which I can tie a piece of clothesline rope on the left side, a sort of rein. And her mane is long and thick. I can tangle my fingers in it and feel secure even at a canter. She is small enough that I can sort of steer her with my hands and my seat, and unlike many ponies, this one has a sweet spirit. She is gentle and tolerant. Sometimes when I fall off she stops and comes back to nudge me with her nose, as if to say *Let's try that again.*

Yes, I told the girl that I rode a good bit, that, in fact, I had studied dressage for several years. She did not ask what that was, and I could tell by the shadow that crossed her face that she didn't know and wasn't going to ask. I asked her if she rode dressage, and she said she rode trails and Western. I told her that I rode English and did a good bit of jumping, three-foot, four-foot, that I was hoping to get good enough to do some three-day eventing. The shadow of ignorance crossed her face again. Then she told me she barrel raced and was going to raise Appaloosas. Real horse talk. I knew I had won.

Her companion asked if I rode bareback much. Of course I said yes, and this was no lie. I had never ridden any other way. But this I did not tell him for he would have known instantly that I was lying about everything else.

"Oh just give her a leg up," the girl had said casually to her friend. I had never had a leg up, but I had read about it in my introductory book on riding and watched as he bent over by the horse's left side and laced his fingers into a stirrup. Self-conscious about putting my knee in the hands of a stranger, yet fearing he would change his mind and deny me the seat on that horse, I knelt the left knee up into his cupped hands, as I read to, and he shot me straight up. I came down on the horse's withers, facing the right direction. I felt the whack of his withers painfully against the bones of my crotch. I felt the horse's surprise. His back dipped a bit acknowledging the added weight. Then he swung his backside around fast, keeping his front hooves in place. His ears flattened and he twisted his head around sharply, like a snake, to snap at my knee.

Tim was getting scared by then and telling me to get off, get off. I was perfectly ready in spirit to comply, but I had never gotten off so big a horse and was not ready to lose face in front of Tim. So instead I murmured and cooed to the horse, slapping at his neck with feigned confidence, and asked what his name was. The horse was shifting around in the lounging shed somewhat less than calmly. He scraped me along a creosote-painted wall beam, the rough wood tearing at my flesh of my knee and calf. Then he backed into the wall and scratched his rump against the splintery wood. I had no control, but as long as the horse's movement stayed minimal, I didn't feel the fear I should have been feeling.

The boy snorted at me, telling me the horses had no names. They were just horses his uncle bought in lots and field-boarded in Mr. Breck's cow pasture until there was a livestock auction. Some got sold for riding, some for dog food and glue. He told me to call my horse Buster.

Buster moved off the wall and out to the middle of shed, then finally stood still, but not calmly. I could feel him quivering. I could feel his hide ripple under my bare thighs. I could sense that he really did not want me on his back any more than I wanted to be there now. But how to get down? The equestrian. The dressage artist. The future cross country eventer.

"Good Buster. Good Buster," I said, and slapped him on the neck again, my hand less significant to him than a green head fly. I did not give a kick to try to make him go. By then my intoxication had faded and I was thinking more clearly again. I wondered about who had owned this horse? Who had ridden him? Tamed him? Loved him? He was, I thought, too beautiful not to have been loved, and with that thought, my madness, the intoxication, surged again; I knew in my heart that this horse, this beautiful beautiful horse was to the uncle and the teens no different than the other twenty or so that dotted the field and hung out in the two lounging sheds. They did not see that he was so dark a bay that he shown black in the sun, that he had a perfect strip of white blaze running evenly from forehead to muzzle. They had not studied him every day for almost a week, learning his every angle, creating for him a long bloodline back to the kings of the Arabian sands, to the King of the Wind himself. His noble brow, his dancing tail.

The boy said something like "Well are you gonna take yourself a ride or not?" Then I heard the loud smack of his open hand on Buster's rump and felt his powerful haunches tuck under him for a mere instant before he bolted out of the shed into the blinding sunlight and August heat to gallop away from the shed and the road and into the field. The pony and I had never galloped.

We are streaking deeper and deeper into the field. I do not like going fast like this. I am not liking this at all and I want to get off. There is nothing to hold on to, no mane, no rope. I think of just throwing myself off, bailing out, but fear keeps me glued where I am. The horse runs full out into a wooded part of the field, on paths made by decades of cows, narrow, uneven, with steep sides, strewn with rocks. He stumbles several time but always regains his balance and returns to his insane pace. I am thinking that if he would just slow down, I would jump. There is no shame here. At one point he lunges up out of the cow path, nothing more than a foot-deep rut, not the place for his long strides and delicate ankles. When he heaves his body onto a narrow slit of a path into a part of the woods where slender trees grow close together, I think he will slow, even halt. But he has no intention of doing either. I cry out "Whoa Buster. Whoa Buster." He ignores me. I can't jump off. I know I will die. I make myself as small as possible and cling, hands pressed into his neck, legs pressed into his shoulders, no doubt inter- fering with his stride and infuriating him further. I do not want to see trees rushing at me and boulders passing so close to my legs. I do not want to see. I close my eyes and wait for whatever happens. I simply want this to end and I want to know I will still be here. I want.

This pleasant cow pasture, a huge seemingly endless space, was always my playground when I spent my requisite week at Uncle Carver's and Aunt Edith's, keeping company with my cousin Tim, always looking for something to do and usually finding it in this cow pasture. The pasture ran from right behind Tim's house out and up to a rise which, after we crossed over it, liberated us from the spying of Tim's older sisters and from the need to indicate we had heard when Aunt Edith called or rang the farm bell. The pasture was flat in some places and carved with gullies and gulches in others. Huge boulders and large flat rocks sat gray against the green of summer grass. Meadow muffins were plentiful, some very new and others dried. Tim and I used to run a sort of race that was won not against time but by being the one *not* to step in a muffin.

Sections of the field were wooded, and woods bordered it on three sides. A wooded area where cows have been is a place of bucolic beauty. Cows graze and walk the grass flat and smooth like moss. The floor of such a woods seems supernaturally clean swept, as if the maintenance of fairies. At about the halfway point towards the back of the field, it began a fast and steep descent to a train track that ran along the Patapsco River, no more than a good-sized creek by that time because of the Liberty Dam. Once paddle-wheel boats and other substantial vessels had travelled the river. And early on, when the train track was finally finished from Baltimore to Ellicott City, a horse and buggy had raced the first train and almost won.

We were forbidden to go down to play in the cool shade near the river because of bums and hobos, the homeless of our childhood. "They steal children and sell them," Aunt Edith would warn us. We went down there a lot, regardless, to play with and around the river, catching crayfish and lizards, enjoying the moist and dank of the spot. The flat land near the river and its banks, not so long before river bottom themselves, were punctuated with smooth rocks, firmly planted in hard ground densely carpeted with mosses. Sometimes we stripped, carefully keeping our clothes near enough by to get to fast, but far enough away so they wouldn't get wet. Then we sat in the shallow running water, making rocks of our knees and sitting still enough that fish would begin to tickle our skin. There was magic there, something both profoundly, even painfully lonely and exultant of pure isolation. We were outside of time, outside of our habitual skins, and at times we would even find ourselves talking free of the rivalry of gender and shared age, talking about the trials of siblings and adults, particularly grandparents, of schools and teachers. Sometimes we would just go and sit, never seeing another human except when a train went through. Then we hid so the conductor would not see us and tell Uncle Carver — we never doubted that all adults knew one another and would report on us.

We saw cows and raccoons, yes. We saw deer and quail, occasionally red fox and wild dogs. More recently horses, too, but we never saw the bums and hobos. This disappointed us.

When the pasture began this descent, it grew rockier and rutted by gullies which channelled runoff in heavy rains. The land became terribly uneven, hard to walk on on foot. It is this descent that Buster and I are making now, out of the woods and going down hill, hell bent, full out, with me thinking, not for the first time in my short life, the thoughts of a person about to die. "No one broke this horse" and "This horse is wild" and "I am going to die painfully" and other such thoughts which created a rather accurate approximation of the moral-of-the-story lecture I will hear all evening. "Miss Betsy, you can't just go into some field and get on some strange horse. The horses aren't yours to begin with and you can't predict what will happen." Aunt Edith will shake her head as she says this, looking sorrowful, wisps of cigarette smoke filtering out of her narrow nostrils.

I already know what can happen, and if God is watching me when Aunt Edith can't, like my Mom has told me God does when *she* can't, then God knows I have really been dumb and bad this time. I should have known better, I think. I did know better. My words before I was hefted onto Buster are much with me. Lies. Liar. Tongue on fire.

Buster veers around a rock and jumps a gully. I almost go off his left side.

I have never had a riding lesson in my eleven and a half years other than those given me by the pony and two books. I hear the lies I told those two teenagers. "I do dressage," I told them. "I can jump a four-foot fence easily," I told them. Actually, I can, but I don't need a horse to do it. I almost started telling them about my own horse, but Tim was there and knew I didn't have one. The rest, though, he can't be sure is a lie. He can suspect, but he can't know. My father has a friend who teaches and trains riders in dressage. For all Tim knows I take lessons from her. I want so much to study with her that sometimes I tell people I have, and I have no reason to doubt that I have told Tim this. Her own father had ridden with the Spanish Riding School in Vienna. She has a Lipizzaner.

Since I have read and reread my two books on horses, I can talk the lingo pretty well. I even know and understand some principles well enough to apply them. I have read every horse story in every library I have had access to. I tell lies about my riding abilities to anyone who will listen and who I think will never find out I am lying. Half the time, I even believe myself. Riding and horses are a sickness with me. I can't think of anything else I lie about or anything else I daydream about as much. Just horses. Sometimes, in the back seat of a car, I imagine myself outside of the car, galloping along handily on some amazing stallion, keeping good time with the car as we head towards our mutual destination. I imagine my bike a horse, willing it to jump small obstacles and sparingly, with clothespins, attaching a few clumps of five or six cards in its spokes to affect the sounds of hooves rather than the rev of engine.

And now I am going to die. I can't remember if lying is one of the deadly sins, but I am sure at this moment it is. Otherwise, why would I be careening down this rugged hill, no brakes, trying to stay on this horse, begging him to stop, begging God for him to stop, making promises about how good I'll be if he stops, confessing to myself the extent of my lies and promising, if I live, *if* I live, to never fabricate on my horse fantasies again except to myself. I will stop will stop will stop. I will stop.

And then with no warning Buster does. As only horses can. From full out to full nothing. I am flying through air and then my cousin, who has followed us somehow, is standing over me telling me to get up, to stop playing like I am asleep. "Remember when we played dead to see if buzzards came?" he yells at me. I can hear fear under anger. I can hear him, but I can't seem to respond. "Well they came," he yells, "You know they came and you were scared. And if they come now, don't expect me to scare them away for you." He yells like this for a while and then he finishes. "Okay. Lie there. I'm going home and I'm going to tell." He stalks off. I hear him leave and it is good to have him stop yelling. But then I hear nothing and fear fills me, seeping into my skin and bones like cold water. I am nauseous. My head is explosive with pain and then, as I begin to take inventory, I realize that something is wrong with my left arm. I realize, too, that my eyes are closed, so I open them. Tim is standing about five feet away looking angry and scared. When our eyes meet, I see him exhale and relax. Everything is alright. I am not dead and he is not in trouble. "Come on," he says. "We have to go home and tell my mother what you did." Somehow I get to my feet.

We are probably no more than a half a mile from Tim's house, but half of that climbs back up the steep rocky terrain. I am not sure I can make it back. I can tell I am very hurt. Vicious waves of nausea nearly topple me. At times I feel like I am seeing through a narrow tube, a toilet paper tube then a paper towel tube. I stop several times to be sick. Tim stops and waits but won't look at me. I tell him my arm is broken. I tell him I have a concussion. He ignores me then and he ignores me later when I ask him if he can go get someone. I want only to lie down on the rough, stony ground and sleep.

"Who?" he asks. And he is right. Who? Who would be there

to come get me and how would they get to me? How would anyone get me out of this pasture? If I lie down here I will be here forever. Tim probably won't even tell them where to find me. I climb and climb, stumbling to my knees regularly, imbalanced by the explosions in my head and the grating aching agony in my upper arm. We reach the top of the hill. My skull is shattered. I am dizzy. Then I am sick again. Tim lets me rest briefly before moving me on.

He finally says that he hadn't known I could ride like that, hadn't believed me, that I was going so fast that he couldn't keep up and had to just follow the hoof prints he thought were my horse's. I think, *Now is a moment when I can begin to be good.* I could tell him he was right not to believe me, that it had been an accident that I hadn't fallen off before the horse got out of the lounging shed. But I just cannot. Tim asks how I fell off. I start to tell him that I had not really fallen off, no; the horse had fallen beneath me, but I stop. By not confessing the whole huge lie to Tim, I have already begun breaking my oath that I will never lie about horses and riding again, so I suck the story that came first to mind back and tell Tim briefly the truth about how I fell off — that the horse had stopped abruptly and I had catapulted over its head. Tim shakes his head and asks if I landed on mine. I don't know, but that would explain the explosions each step makes in my skull.

Once we reach the upper part of the field, I know I can make it. I tell Tim again that my arm is broken. He asks how I know. I just know, I tell him. "Can you wiggle your fingers?" he asks. I can, so he says it's not broken. Besides, he adds, "You'd be crying if it were broken." He is right that I haven't cried. But he is wrong to think that is significant. I never cry under circumstances like this. When I am injured or in trouble, the frightened part of me withdraws and the part that stays behind copes with what has to be coped with. I will cry later when everything is over. But not in front of Tim.

Eventually we get to the final obstacles — two rows of barbed wire fence, the outer fence about eighteen inches beyond the inner fence. Each fence has three strands. The first fence is electrified to turn cattle back. Cows will walk down any fence if they want something on the other side. The electricity urges them to think again. It doesn't necessarily stop them.

Usually I can negotiate this complex fencing with ease, but today doing so seems impossible. The gate nearest to Tim's house hangs another half mile away in the opposite direction, near the house of the pasture's owner. Too far to even consider, particularly when just on the other side of these rusted barbed strands sits Tim's house. Both of us want only to be in that house. Tim helps me through the fences as much and as gently as a person can help with a barbed wire fence, but when I finally find myself on the other side, I am slightly singed and definitely torn by barbs. The back of my green Girl Scout tee shirt has practically been torn from my back. I am bleeding here and there from barb scratches, and I don't care.

For Tim, all is well now. He hands me over to his mother and fades from the scene, though not out of hearing. He expects she will give me what for and has said as much repeatedly throughout our trek. I followed his threats like promises. Getting what for would return life to normal. But she doesn't yell at me. She shakes her head and makes clicking sounds. She says, for the first time that evening, "Miss Betsy, you can't just go into some field and get on some strange horse. The horses aren't yours to begin with and you can't predict what will happen." I sit on a stool in the bathroom while she leans over me and cuts away the remaining shreds of my tee shirt, a smoking cigarette caught between her lips. She is one who has always called me Miss Betsy, and I have always felt singled out by that Miss as someone who was trouble, someone who was too everything. When she asks me what happened, I mumble a simple recounting of what happened. She draws me a hot bath in the old deep tub. I am filthy, she tells me. I feel like dust and smell like dirty sweat and vomit. There is company coming for dinner. I tell her, finally, that I think I have broken my arm. She asks, as did Tim, if I can wiggle my fingers. When I show her that I can, she dismisses the possibility of a break and leaves me to my bath.

I sit in the tub nearly asleep when the door opens, no knock, and cooler air cuts the steamy warmth of the bathroom. Uncle Carver comes in, home from work early because of me. Aunt Edith called him.

As he looks me over, I feel conscious of beginning breasts and my general nudity. It's nothing he says or does, just my sudden awareness that other than my father, he is the only adult male who has ever come into the bathroom when I was bathing. Finally he asks me to move my fingers, which I do, and he tells me the arm can't be broken. It is not even swollen or bruised. He pats my head, setting off a blast of pain, and leaves, letting in more cool air as he goes. I go back to my dozing until one of Tim's sisters comes for me. She is fifteen and once, when five or six, was nearly killed by a car when it came round a bend too fast and hit her on her bike. She knows pain and is very gentle with me.

Because there is company for dinner, I must dress. Tim's sister helps me dress. She realizes, as we work at getting me in panties and slip, that I cannot raise my left arm at the shoulder

hardly at all, much less over my head. Very carefully we manage
to get me into the only dress I brought with me. It is my favorite
dress, vines of large deep blue and dark burgundy flowers and
green leaves on a fawn background. Its dropped-waist skirt
flares slightly at the hips. The rest of the dress, neck to where
the skirt begins, is straight and narrow. Torturous. After several
false starts, my cousin finally arranges the dress on the floor
and has me step into its center; then she carefully pulls it up
my body and even more carefully pulls the left sleeve up my
injured arm. I tell her I think the arm is broken. She says her
father does not think so and tells me to be glad there's nothing
broken. She brushes my hair. She tells me that broken bones
hurt more than anything. I guess she knows, after getting hit
by a car. But suddenly I feel certain again. I know without
doubt that my arm is broken and I am tired of no one believing
me. In retrospect, they might have been afraid to believe. I had
been in their charge for a week. It should not, I am sure they
believed, have been possible for it to happen. In reality, they
could no more have protected me from my obsession with
horses than they would, a year or so later, be able to protect
Tim from blowing off some fingers in his effort to make a
rocket that would soar. The only fuel he could find was gun-
powder.

Dinner — a blur of dark dining room, filled with the clatter
of silver on china and the chatter of adults. I cannot not eat.
Mild nausea continues in waves. At some points in the meal I
can hardly sit up straight or stay awake. At other moments, I
am sharply lucid, angry and hurting. At all moments I am
silent, refusing to answer the questions I am asked. I am teased,

and finally I am rude. Aunt Edith has had enough and, taking me by my good shoulder, leads me upstairs to her room to tell me that if I can't behave, she is going to call my mother and father and tell them I can't behave. I know she means this as a threat, but I tell her very honestly that I don't think I can behave. She dials the phone and tells whoever answers that I have had "a little accident" that day and wasn't behaving very "grown up about it." The she hands me the phone and tells me to tell my mother what I've done, standing beside me as I recount the story and finally tell my parents that I think my left arm is broken. She believes me even though Aunt Edith has warned her that I think my arm is broken and assured her that it's not. My mother asks if I want them to come and bring me home.

I remember that wait for them as extremely long, a wait when I was conscious of each minute, each second. When they do arrive, a little more than an hour later, they find me packed and waiting, by choice, on a straight chair just inside the front door. I am still in my fancy dress.

Before leaving the house they had called our family doctor. They came armed with pillows. My father drove and my mother sat with me in the back seat, keeping my arm immobilized and cushioned with pillows, keeping me from falling asleep in case I was concussed, getting me to tell my story over and over. I did not include one bit of untruth. Once home and packed with pillows into bed, they continued to wake me up at short intervals with this or that question, and the next day, as my mother drove into Annapolis for x-rays, I observed for the first time how very many railroad crossings the car had to stumble over. The x-rays are handled by a man who, because my fingers can wiggle, joins the disbelievers until he gets the shot just right. From behind his lead wall, my mother and I hear him bark in disbelief, "Dear Mother Mary Mother of Our Lord. I have never seen a break like this." From the hospital we stumble over cobblestones on our way to the doctor who will fix me up.

Broken right through into the shoulder joint, my arm bone was also shattered on the outer side. Some bone was even turned to powder, *pulverized,* Dr. Bullman said. And there was a dent. Buster's hoof had, unintentionally I was and remain sure, connected hard as he raced past me and continued downhill. While some horses might with joy step on a person's foot during grooming, horses generally won't intentionally trample a person. Buster had not kicked me in the head. I had simply whacked it hard and solidly on a rock. The doctor taped me, the upper arm tightly to my side and my lower arm bent so that left my hand rested on my chest, looking for all the world like a broken wing. The tape practically covered my upper torso, and while the fracture healed, I wore oversized shirts with the left sleeve pinned like the sleeves of amputees.

Sixth grade began for me with much embarrassment. Instead of winning me some sort of prestige, my broken arm's presentation, *sans* cast, won me banter about how much my "boobs" had grown. One of my cleverer classmates called me the Hunchbreast of Notre Dame, and the new title caught on fast. A cast would have been cool. My teacher that year started school with a cast and let us all sign it that first day. A few days later, she told the class her story, laughing goodnaturedly at her silliness as she told us that she had simply lost her footing coming down the steps of the National Gallery and broken her ankle. When she then turned to me and invited me to tell my story, I embellished and fabricated a tale of horror and bravery and, of course, great equestrian skill. I kept us in the dangerous, rugged field, but I linked my ride that day to my practicing, yes, to become a cross country, three-day event rider. I described with great detail the tall stone wall jump at which the horse had balked and sent me flying over first. I described how, even already injured, I had managed to move almost, but not quite, out of the way when my steed followed me over the wall, landing on my arm. And my arm, well it had been broken in so many places that a cast had been impossible. I quoted the x-ray technician's exclamation, but attributed it to the doctor who, never having encountered such a break, had had to tape my arm to me so as to completely immobilize it. Lies, yes, but the lies served a good purpose. Some of my peers made less fun of my pinned left sleeves on my oversized shirts. My teacher told me that I told a good story, that maybe I'd be a writer when I grew up.

I look back on this era of horse lies and self-recreation and shake my head, wondering — as my grandparents and teachers had wondered so many times — where my mind *was*. I remember too that I had a great hatred of not being believed when I was telling the truth. The day my arm was formally declared broken, I felt exonerated and noble. When my mother and I got back to the house, I asked her to call Aunt Edith and *tell* her I had been right. I felt righteous and affirmed. The irony of this contradiction was not lost on me even then. After the phone call, and after a meal of creamed spinach on toast with slices of hard boiled egg, I lay on our living room sofa looking at the piano I would be unable to play for a while, feeling my arm throb and throb, and hearing the good me chastising. "Liar liar pants on fire. Remember the boy who cried wolf. Remember Pinocchio's nose. Remember, once people know someone is a liar, they never believe anything that person says, ever again." I remember wanting to ask my mother and father how to stop my lying about my skill with horses, but though I knew they could understand how I might have gone into that field and gotten on that horse and gone for that race and gotten hurt, I thought that had I confessed to my manipulation of the situation with lies, they would have been angry.

But there is something more to some lying than just telling untruths. Sometimes people lie not because they are wicked but because they want so much to be wonderful in some way that is denied them by their lives' circumstances. They lie because they do not like themselves as they are, and they need to revise their histories, perhaps in hopes of revising their futures. I have a friend, for example, whose need to be exotic, special beyond special, has made herself known for living a full life, a hard life, and known as a survivor of long suffering that has accompanied her from childhood into adulthood. She told me many years ago that she had been married at fifteen to a drug dealer, had had his child, and that he had been killed in a meth or heroin deal gone sour and the baby had died in an automobile accident with her dead husband's parents. Now this had the ring of a lie to it the moment I heard it, and years later, married and having her first child in this marriage, she never spoke of her pregnancy as if it were any other than her first. She got books for first-time mothers and read them like a first-time mother. Pregnant with her second son, she spoke like a veteran. Both times, I resisted the urge to ask her about the story she had told me about her life at fifteen, though someday I might — some day when we both have grown so fully into ourselves that we can come face-to-face with the selves we have fabricated and, without shame, examine the lengths we have gone at various times in our lives to be special beyond special.

Baptism V
Gloria Sings

"These boots are made for walking." Gloria has a mike and mike stand in the middle of the basement playroom. Beside the mike stand is an apple crate that she puts her right foot on as she sways and sings badly into the mike. "These boots were made for walkin' and that's just what they'll doooooo. One of these days these boots are gonna walk right over you-oo — oo." Where the bass lick would start, she sings, "Gaagaa gaagaa gaagaa gaagaa gaadum gaadum gaadum gaadum. Gaagaa gaagaa gaagaa gaagaa gaadum gaa gaa gaa." She can sing the whole Nancy Sinatra album, lyrics and licks alike. She can sing through her Sonny and Cher and Petula Clark albums. I am twelve and paid to watch her, sit her, and I don't know how to play with her, but she gives me forceful directions, yelling out avid instructions. I just follow them.

"Stomp stomp stomp!" she yells when she's singing "These Boots." "Stomp stomp stomp!" So I stomp back and forth in front of her as though she is on a stage and I am dancing, but if I do dance, she yells "Stomp! Don't dance! Stomp!" So I stomp.

Sometimes Gloria yells for me to sing and if I get a word wrong she stops and corrects me. How she can hear me over her own volume I do not know, but she can. "Not 'going to.' It's *gonna gonna*. Say *gonna*, Betsy."

"Gonna Betsy," I respond, but she doesn't get the joke.

"*Not* gonna Betsy just *gonna*." So I behave, singing "gonna" instead of "going to" and "walkin'" instead of "walking" and "wonna" instead of "one of." It interests me that she hears so distinctly the nuances of pronunciation when she herself cannot pronounce words so well. She calls me something more like Bezzy than Betsy. Without the syntax of lyrics, her own sentences are jumbled. In fact, she often tries to get by with one or two words and body gestures. Sometimes, if I don't get her point fast enough, she will simply pick me up and take me where she wants me to be and plunk me down. Other times, if I make her too happy, she will simply pick me up and squeeze me till I think I might pass out. I try, when I sit her, to walk a fine line between wrong and too right. But I rarely make it through any time with her without some hoisting and hugging. She's fast. She's huge. And can move as silently as a cat when she wants. One of her favorite games at the beach is to sneak up the high dive and grab me from behind and fling me out into space. Then she will come cannonballing down and God help me if she hasn't flung me far enough out because I usually land splat on the surface of the river and get the wind knocked out of me. She terrifies me, but her mother asks me to sit for her because I am one of the few people Gloria likes, probably because I pay extreme attention to her every move, obey her every whim, and don't talk back.

If Gloria wants to eat a bag of Hydrox, Gloria eats a bag of Hydrox. If she wants to take all the Hydrox apart and only eat the cream centers, she does that too. I wait until she is finished and put the chocolate cookies parts back in the bag. One day she made me cook her an entire package of hot dogs. She wanted me to do it on her father's charcoal grill. I told her I didn't have matches and didn't know how to cook on a grill, but she said, "Is easy," and searched futilely for matches everywhere. I boiled the hot dogs in the end and warmed their rolls in the oven. Gloria never offers me a single bite of whatever it is she eats. Food is very important to her, her mother tells me, and it keeps her busy.

In a very real way, Gloria is easier to sit than real kids because if her mother comes home and finds a bag of Hydrox without centers or a package of hot dogs and hot dog rolls gone, she doesn't blame it on me. If she comes home and finds Gloria, swaying and swinging with her mike stand, singing topless, her large breasts and stomach jumping up and down and jiggling as I stomp around in front of her singing "Gaagaa gaagaa gaagaa gaagaa gaadum gaadum gaadum gaadum," her mother doesn't tell me I should not have let her take her shirt and bra off. When I tell her mother the first time I sit that my sitting fee is fifty cents an hour, she says, "I think we can do a little better than that" and pays me three dollars an hour, a fact I keep secret from other potential sitters, though I doubt their mothers would allow them to take the job. Gloria is a challenge. I don't think my own mother would let me were she able to find some way to say no to Gloria's mother that would not reflect on Gloria. She worries that Gloria might hurt me. I am careful to avoid her hurting me, but she usually manages to in some minor way, even if only with a glancing hug.

Gloria is twenty-one when her parents move near us and twenty-three when they move elsewhere. Gloria is "old for someone with her problem" her mother tells me. "Most people like her die in their teens," I learn from a neighbor. I wouldn't know. I do not know anyone else like Gloria. She has several older brothers and sisters, five or six as far as I can figure it. For some reason, asking questions about Gloria and her family is something my vague social instincts suggest I not do. Her mother and father both tell me that she is their last, their youngest, their angel who will never leave home.

So what Gloria wants, Gloria gets, but she does not want much. The mike and stand, the amplifier, a cheap guitar, her records and record player, Hydrox, hot dogs, and me stomping or spinning on command add up to a pretty good day for her. She asked her mother for me to be her sitter when we met at the beach one day. Gloria can swim well, after a fashion. The day we met I was swimming laps. June, I was on the swim team and practicing and I swam smack into her. She had put herself in my lane. I broke stroke and back paddled, seeing her wet head and hearing her laugh. "You swim good," she said. She introduced herself and I myself and she talked some, in her own way, about her records and mike, treading water, powerfully churning a whirlpool around her. Then suddenly she surged forward and pushed my head under. The games began. I dove low and avoided her large rotating feet. I swam under her and made it to the pier. When I surfaced at the ladder, behind her, I had to make a choice. Be polite and let her know where I was or slip up onto the pier and head for shore. The decision was a slow and conscious one, hard. What I wanted to do was leave, but I was old enough, almost twelve, and I recognized Gloria, though childlike, as an adult. I called her name and I was hers.

The only thing Gloria wants that no one can give her is a man's love. She understands wanting a man, wanting kisses. She understands wanting more than kisses. Wanting none of that myself, I try to avoid this topic. But during our two years of knowing each other, it comes up more and more in increasingly more embarrassing detail.

"Well I think I'm going out of my head, Yes I think I'm going out of my head, Over you — oo-oo, Over you-oo-oo. I want you . . . to want me . . . I need you so badly I can't think of anything but you . . ." As Gloria sings this song, she wraps herself around her mike stand and closes her eyes tight. On a day when she's really focused on love, she'll sing song after song till she exhausts herself and falls to the floor laughing and rolling. While I am ordered to stomp with "These Boots," she orders me to spin with "Out of My Head" and walk around in a circle going "Ahhh" with "The Girl from Ipanema." I am always glad when Gloria collapses for she exhausts me, though when she stops singing, I never know what will come next. More songs? Cookies? Talk? Not talk really, but cross examination, to this effect.

"Do you have a boyfriend, Bezzy?" No, I don't. But if I answer no, sometimes she'll ask why not and I'll tell her I am not that crazy about boys. Other times she'll get angry and tell me that I *do* have one. "Say 'I do', Bezzy, like you're getting married." She'll chortle at that. Then she'll laugh out loud a lot telling me to say "I do" until I give in and say "I do. I have a boyfriend," and then she wants to know what his name is and where he lives and if he kisses me and if he kisses me with his tongue and if, well, "You know," she'll say, and I'll find myself answering more and more of her questions about a boyfriend I don't have and discovering that any answer is a potential mine. "Don't say he doesn't kiss you!" So I revise my story. "Okay, he kisses me."

"With his tongue," she yells and laughs, and I give in and say "Yes he kisses me with his tongue," thinking only of one creepy cousin who, when we visit, is told to "Give your cousin Betsy a kiss" and who rebels by getting close and licking the tip of my nose. He always does that and yet his mother never fails to demand that he give me a kiss.

I revise and revise till Gloria's fantasy about my boyfriend pleases her. I revise this boyfriend, fleshing him out — he has to be older than Gloria, twenty-six ideally and blond but like Sonny Bono but with a voice like John Sebastian and he has to take me downtown to parties. Gloria sings "Downtown," where the lights and signs are pretty, when she tells me this.

Three dollars an hour or not, after two years of sitting Gloria I am glad when her parents and she move away, them encouraging me to come visit, me promising "Oh I will" and knowing I won't. But a year later, when "G-L-O-R-I-A" hits the charts and "Let's Spend the Night Together" is banned from the radio waves, I can see Gloria and her mike stand and hear her shouting out her lyrics as vividly as if she were in the same room, and I remember her singing "Do you believe in magic in a young girl's heart," and then yelling "Do you Bezzy? Do you believe in magic in a young girl's heart?"

Before
the Storm

I am driving home from work. I pause where I turn up the hill from the river road to my house to let an oncoming car pass. As it does, I recognize the sound of the car so sharply that I almost feel the pelvic vibration of its V-8. I see the dark racing stripes where its chrome trim has fallen away from its dull matte black finish. Its roof is ragged, a ruffle of peeling pale vinyl. I have ridden in that car in another time, in another decade, another state, when I was young and the car I rode in was as old then as the growling 1970 Duster that crosses my path in this thick sultry summer dusk. I know as sharply as if I were in that Duster that in the passengers' compartment sex charges the air like the sharp ozone breath of lightning, even if the act of sex is not yet a reality between the dark haired girl and her blond escort, even if they cannot yet *name* that tension that holds them polarized on either side of that front seat, the tension that presses her against the passenger door and him against the driver's. Does she grasp the handhold in the arm rest, her slender fingers wrapped around tight? Does she wear her seatbelt? In my day, cars that rumbled like earthquakes beneath our thighs did not usually have working safety belts. And him? Blond hair cut longish and even as if with a bowl — he seems to hang from the wheel, left hand ten o'clock, right hand two. What would happen if he were to lean back into his seat, hold the wheel only with the left hand at nine o'clock, leaving his right hand free to reach across the seat? Would she take his hand? Have seat belts and bucket seats ruined the romance of the road?

They pass. I turn up my hill. I am not embarrassed that I transport myself so blithely, curiously into others' lives and loins. They have deflected the unpleasant gaze of my thoughts and I had been thinking hard, imagining in thunderous silent quakes a terribly violent suicide attempt I learned of a few hours before, a man I've known forever, now in mid-life and disappointed by his life, by love, by himself. He tried to slit his own throat. All afternoon since I learned this I have sat squat, pulling my neck down between my shoulders, like a turtle or a vulture. I ring my neck with my fingers and cupped hands.

Before any storm of note, the surface of the river darkens, flushes as if in anger from rich milk chocolate to austere bitter-sweet. Then it picks up a choppy rhythm, flippant peaks of water flicking faster and faster, trembling, then dancing, then spinning, then frothing into peaks, whipped cream, till all sweetness gives way to anger and rain drives sharp into the face of any fool still afloat, and white caps flail in fury, slapping a small skiff off its course. By then the water, a black licorice ribbon path, merges with rain and clouds into one dark wall. Only streaks of lightning illuminate the way home. The lone young boater, who chances to be in the small skiff still out of sight of mooring, casts hope aside and acknowledges death, an acknowledgement which makes one oddly calm and intelligent.

I want to write, here, about love.

Angus St. Barrone is far too young for me and thus just right because I am far too young for myself. There is some hunger between us, but we have no name for it, simply an unvoiced shared desire to be near each other, alone. A summer storm is ending. August. In two days, Angus and his family are moving away from this part of the river, further down stream into a bigger house that they've had built specially. I have promised to visit. By boat or bike a visit is possible from my point of view. But this day I sit at his kitchen table, waiting for him to come downstairs from packing to engage with me in what is probably our last play, and I tell his mother that they are not moving far and that I will visit. I probably seem cocky. I think I often did seem cocky, though I wasn't. She asks me not to visit, says Angus will be going to a new school, will need to make new friends. She sings me the first two lines of "Auld Lang Syne" and explains the song, telling me that we all need to leave people behind. She makes it sound like I am doing the leaving, like I am doing the right thing, but I know I am being left. Then Angus comes and we go out into the end of a storm that has lost its rage and we head to the beach and the pier and, yes, it is empty of all people and, yes, as we hoped, the pier is submerged under two inches of water.

There has been a lot of rain this week, a pattern we know well enough to make us hope for the pier under a carpet of water. We head out that carpet's length and, invisible as the pier is, to any observer we must look like nymphs walking on water. The wood planks of the pier are slick from a week of storms and the constant lubrication of whatever other possible liquids the wood has absorbed — mineral oil, Coppertone, dog drool, fish drippings and eel slime, algae, melted fat from old chicken backs used for crab bait, the gelatinous strands of the immense stinging sea nettles we kids all like to dip from the water and fry to a crisp on metal-capped piling tops and the white edges of the pier planks.

At the end of the pier, Angus and I sit down and let our feet rest on the racing dive platform. We let our legs float up and we lie back onto the pier, letting go of its edge and drifting off into the deep.

Why is this magic? This submerged pier, this unity of shallow and deep water, a seamless line of shallow and deep, a phenomenon of a series of storms. In our own worlds, not each other's, we glide on and off the pier like seals, like otter, the orca and dolphin at Sea World in Orlando. We are silent. There exists nothing to say. But eventually we again sit side-by-side on the pier, elbows touching, feet resting on the racing platform. We are comfortable and silent and sad. It is almost time to go and I know that I will not see him again. Tomorrow, my parents are taking us on a driving vacation, the theme "caves" — the route south to Virginia and Luray and from there basically unknown until we are home again. Angus is going into fifth grade; I am going into sixth. He is ten; I am eleven. I pat his shoulder lightly and tell him I will miss him. He doesn't respond. Finally, I turn to look at him and ask, "Will you miss me?" His face is wet. River? Tears? He puts his hand on my shoulder and pulls me forward. He kisses me lightly on my cheek. Startled, I pull away and glide into the water, diving deep and long and surfacing to see Angus halfway to the shore end of the pier, running awkwardly on the slippery, submerged boards. I never see him again except in this memory. I feel the quick kiss on my cheek for several months afterwards. I feel the juncture of shallow and deep. I see him halfway down the pier to shore and running. In 1978, I name one of a litter of kittens Angus. My father laughs. The cat is black and white. He thinks I've named it after a brand of scotch. My younger sister names Angus's brother Flower after the skunk in Bambi. I am twenty-five and I still have not forgotten that boy and his kiss at the end of that pier fourteen years before. So I name a cat for Angus of the kiss, his dark hair, his skin white even after a summer of sun and river. His eyes blue. I am sure they were blue.

After Angus is gone, another family moves in. The husband is a descendant of a famous writer, so I seek out his works and read them. I am in sixth grade. Soon, they need a babysitter and my mother and grandmother vouch for me. My older sister, the neighbors' first choice, is beyond babysitting. Indeed, though I will not understand her work till later, she is busy as an artist with an advertising company and is designing such things as the cover of Bob Dylan's *Highway 61 Revisited*. I baby-sit on trial for Billy, who is two and Peter, who is four. We get on fine. My little sister, Kathy, is five and playing with them is like playing with her. Sometimes, I take her with me for the early hours — dinner, Candy Land, tickling, Dr. Seuss. Then my mother comes, takes my sister home to her own bed and I take Billy and Peter to theirs. After that, the job loses its energy. I read and wait, read and wait, try to stay awake. These are people who stay out late, often till two in the morning. They drive all the way to Washington, D.C., for dinner and opera or symphonies or theater.

Television reception is poor in our community, and there is no way for me to know what's on. I sift through their kitchen cabinets where they store foods, boxed and canned goods. There are tins of octopus and smoked oysters. There are small vials of capers and green peppercorns. There are exotic soups in both cans and paper packets — leek, morel, abalone chowder, peanut. There are tiny whole pickles and anchovies, balsamic, tarragon, and shallot vinegars. There is nothing like I would find on my parents' shelves at home. No fruit cocktail, B&M baked beans, Peter Pan peanut butter, cherry Jell-o, Campbell's soup in tomato, mushroom, Scotch broth. No Junket. In my ice box, we have colby cheese and presliced brick cheese. In the my neighbors' ice box, there is brie and camembert, gouda and boucheron. I taste anything that's opened and learn a great deal.

Eventually, after I pass the test of good babysitter, even successfully and gently managing their postman-eating, long-haired, imported German shepherd, I begin to arrive to find dinner waiting to be cooked, not already prepared. I learn to make a white sauce from instructions Peter's and Billy's mother carefully writes out. I learn to flavor it with thinly sliced mushrooms and cooking sherry, thicken it, and serve it over small lamb chops, two for Billy, three for Peter, four for me. In return, perhaps out of defense of my own culinary history, I sometimes make a pie from scratch and leave it. I know how to cook. I need her to know this.

In the spring of 1965, after Billy drowns while I am at school, his mother goes away. I'm not sure where though what I overhear makes clear that her disappearance is directly related to Billy's death. I imagine her in a convent like one I have recently visited with a group from my church. I imagine her in jail. The judgment then amongst neighbors was that her too-free ways with such young children led directly to Billy's drowning. I remember her often at a desk, pen poised over paper. I wonder now if she was a writer. I never knew what either of them did. I never really knew what most adults did unless I saw them at it and it was something I understood. Whatever the reason, she is gone. And the first summer is easy.

Peter's father leaves at 7:30 in the morning and I stay until he gets home. There are no longer recipes to follow for special meals. Some of the cans in the closets begin to rust. Peter's father leaves the cooking up to me, whatever I want to make from whatever ingredients are in the refrigerator. Several times, though, he leaves flour and fruit on the counter, message obvious. He needs a pie. A little in love with him, I make one without fail and leave it untouched on the counter where he had left its ingredients.

Peter and I fall into a good rhythm; my younger sister adds daily to our harmony. Together she and I eat breakfast with Peter and play, doze and play, eat lunch and swim and play some more. During this time, though I am mostly the leader, we are three children set free from adults, magically of an age, learning each other's nuances and intelligences, respectful and loving. We read and go out in my canoe and crab and swim again. The summer is idyllic. During the day, my sister most always at my side, sisterhood transforms from mere siblings to real friends. Then at night, both children in their separate homes and beds, fed and asleep for the night, I resurface to age twelve and begin to learn the luxury of time predictably uninterrupted as I wait for Peter's father to come home.

That summer ends. I continue to sit for Peter during the next school year. His mother remains absent and his father is often late. I begin to assume that she is gone for good. When the next summer comes I am thirteen and this sad duo of father and son have become a solid part of my daily life. Yet while this summer proceeds as the last, I am different. Restless. I am conscious of feeling confused a lot of the time.

I buy my first rock records, and I buy them for the way they make my bones and veins and muscles feel. I purposefully walk nearly two miles to a record store in a new and isolated row of four attached shops along the Ritchie Highway, an early strip, mall surrounded by field, and I buy two albums, *The Electric Comic Book* by the Blues Magoos and *Between the Buttons* by the Rolling Stones. At this time, at least for me, both are equal in status. I want certain songs and these groups offer them. *Gloria.* G-L-O-RIA, Gloooor — ee — ah. Though a Stones song, I do not know this and find it on the Magoo's album. *Let's Spend the Night Together. Ruby Tuesday.* I put the records on my mono suitcase portable player and dance around the room that was my older sister's, undulating and spinning not so differently than she had a mere year before. With her married, the whole second floor is mine now and it teaches me secrecy and freedom. I discover 45s. *Red Rubber Ball. Wipe*

Out. I play them over and over, singing and memorizing words and guitar riffs.

The summer comes and I resume days of babysitting. This summer also brings Peter's father's younger brother, Nate. He is sixteen and, after a few days' distress at having the peace of Peter's house disrupted by someone who seems to have nothing to do but hang around, my irritation does an about-face and I fall in love. I am sure it's love. I swoon through the summer. To dress cool, mod, I take to wearing the same plaid shirt and striped shorts day after day. At home I am sure I am a babble of Nate this, Nate that. At Peter's, I boss Nate around, making clear that his ignorance about cleaning a fish or netting a crab astonishes me. He affably goes along with anything Peter and I want to do. Then he leaves and I spend a lot of my free time skimming across the surface of the Severn on Peter's father's Sunfish howling the lyrics to "Black is Black" into the wind I catch as I race across the surface of the river. I sing about wanting back *my baby*. What does this *mean* to me? At home later, chopping vegetables, I prattle, telling my mother that I am going to rebuild a Model A, like Nate, and learn to fly a plane, like Nate, and spend a summer in Provence, like Nate, and go to Harvard, like Nate. Nothing is impossible and I am going to do it all. Like Nate.

Then seventh grade begins and I find my first girlfriend. She is two years older and ready for love. Suddenly I am part of a group of friends, mixed friends. I become the youngest of a group of fifteen. Suddenly I notice that there are boys I'd never noticed or that boys I'd always known are noticeable. My gaze is a moveable crush, first Pat, now Bryan, then Richard, now Ron, then back to Pat. No one notices. My girlfriend and Ron become attached and they choose their song, one by the

Turtles, *Imagine me and you, I do, I think about you every night, it's only right, to think about the one you love, and hold her tight, so happy together.* I want a boy with whom I can share our own song. But who? When? Pat is in love with Stina and Stina is in love with Jeff. Pat plays Gary Lewis and the Playboys' "This Diamond Ring" over and over if we let him get control of the record player, over and over in the background, *Who wants to buy this diamond ring? She took it off her finger, now it doesn't mean a thing.* Pat is only fifteen. What does this song *mean* to him?

I try out crush after crush. Almost all the boys are possibilities, yet shift and change dance partners as they do, there are always fifteen of us and I am always the fifteenth. And in a conscious way, I am relieved. It is heady and painful enough to be singed by my friends' hormones. I listen to my girlfriend's worries and desires, so huge, so end of the world. "Does he love me? Do you think he loves me?" becomes the chant, the rhythm, the engine driving our lives. I spend hours shaking my head slowly back and forth, responding "I don't know. I don't know. I don't know," a response I will hear myself make to many friends, both men and women, tormented by love, as the next thirty years pull me forward. I carry secret messages between Andrew and Phyllis, between Meredith and John. I spy on Steve for Marianne and Diane who share a crush on him and fear he is in love with the terrible Robin, a boy stealer. I feel sophisticated and immune some days, ugly and undesirable others. On these latter days I regress and, sometimes with one or two of the other girls who are, like me, little more to boys than targets for stones, vent my frustration through pranks or escapes. We leave a six-foot black snake in a shoe box on the desk of our least favorite teacher. We canoe to the mouth of the river, where it mingles with the bay, and then we canoe back, eighteen miles round trip. We sit and throw stones high up into the dusk and watch bats dive to investigate. We make a pact, an anti-boy trust. We invest our love in *men*. Nan takes William Shatner; Suz goes for Leonard Nimoy. I take Lee Majors in his role as Heath in *The Big Valley*. Oddly, we are content, at peace. The storm swirls around us or up ahead of us. We are the calm.

Just before I move to Pennsylvania, Ron's brother takes me to a dance at the Severn School for Boys. My girlfriend goes with Ron, Stina now with Pat, Bryan with Phyllis, Alexander with Marianne. They are all veterans of these dances. This is my first non-cotillion dance. We are not made to fox trot or waltz. We slow dance and frug. I am five-four; Ron's brother is six-four. Stina periodically spotlights us, shrilling like a drunk, over and over, "Oh, they are so CUTE. He's so TALL and she's so SHORT." My ear comes to his heart. I don't quite dare to rest my ear there and listen to its beat. I don't care if Stina is trying to embarrass me or not. The band plays something slow and I am wearing a straight sheath dress, no bodice-and-full-skirt dress and somehow I am suddenly sleek and streamlined, dancing with a boy who *asked* me to a dance. Somehow I know how to fit into his arms, not too close, not too far. Between dances, we stand awkwardly. No hand-holding. No touching at all. Maybe some punch. He keeps saying he is very thirsty and dashing to the punch table. Nothing for any parent to worry about at all.

Until the music begins again.

Storms. Recently, a friend of mine's marriage of twenty-five years has been run ashore hard by her husband's mid-life crisis and resultant affair with a married woman. My friend knew this was happening without knowing, Polanyi's tacit knowledge, unprovable but certain nonetheless. Her anguish has left her red-eyed and thin, sleepless and ever in motion, mysterious like the dark river waters clucking by in the night. Her daughter, eighteen, finally demanded an explanation for why her mother, usually so joyful and present, was drifting around the house, crying a silent current, constantly liquid and murky. Against her own better judgment, my friend told her daughter the truth, to which her daughter said, both in dismay and in the wise disgust of the young, "That's what people do in *high* school. Adults aren't supposed to act like that."

The storm once underway moves on, does not end. Behind it often follows a chain of various storms, squalls with whirl-winds, tempests groaning of torrents and wind, mother storms truly gentle with rains that fall straight down and neither flood the river nor undercut its shores. For a while there may be calm without upheaval, but the storm always seems to return, swelling out hearts and sending our blood surging through our veins, eddying our hopes. Love is one of nature's elemental forces.

Just before Thanksgiving of 1996, my grandmother on my father's side managed to get her heart broken. Yet again. My father and his brother warned her, like sons in their seventies will, grumbling, castigating her about her judgment. They told her the man was no good and that he was going to take what he could from her and then leave her. But still, my grandmother took up with that man living in her part of a senior citizens' community. The man's wife had gone into the hospital and he dramatized it, telling my grandmother he was sure his wife would die, asking where that would leave him, answering his own question, "Just alone," his children hardly ever visiting and yes, she agreed yes, the children hardly ever visit and she was alone too and yes if they stuck together they would yes not be alone. Yes. So they took up with each other, "smoochin' and hoochin' in the halls" she brazenly bragged to my father and uncle. "She had him in her *room*," my father tells my mother, and my mother and I shake our heads, at first when my father is not looking, later with him once he sees the humor. My grandmother was ninety-four years old, then. Her lover was eighty-eight. My father and his brother refer to him as "that dirty old man."

"At least they won't get pregnant," my mother observes. I snicker. But there are worse things in love. The man's wife recovers and comes home and he tells my grandmother that he cannot see her anymore, but my grandmother is persistent, chases him, will not give up, refuses to eat, cries in public, wails over the phone to my father and my uncle. They go to see her and go to see her. She is inconsolable, particularly when that dirty old man's son, in his seventies like my father and uncle, helps move his father and mother to another place in the same senior home because that "shameless hussy," who is my grandmother, just won't give up. Love relents not. Even months later she will rewrite the truth to perpetuate her dream of love — the box of chocolate-dipped, pistachio candies for which my father stands an hour in line to buy her for Christmas, the dozen red roses my parents send for her January birthday, *all*, she believes, are from *him*. She knows. She *knows* he is courting her still, says he is a gentleman, not rushing her. She forgets about the wife. She looks for him daily and nightly, remembering how together they slow-danced in the halls, remembering their negotiation of aluminum walkers.

I wonder what song of love they shared. I wonder what song of love lost she hums solo now. I wonder too if, while washed ashore by this particular gale, she watches the horizon for another lone soul upon whom she will direct her gaze like the light at the end of a pier, beckoning, reeling him in before the next storm.

To Feel the Cords that Bind

I find surcease from the entanglement of questions only when I concede that I am not obliged to know everything. In a world where many desperately seek to know all the answers, it is not very popular to believe, and then state, I do not need to know all things. I remind myself that it is sufficient that I know what I know and know that without believing that I will always know what I know or that what I know will always be true.

Maya Angelou,
Wouldn't Take Nothing for My Journey Now

To stick your hands into the river is to feel the cords that bind the earth together in one piece.

Barry Lopez,
River Notes

Crossing
with Deer
at Providence Road

As much as I remember I also forget. Scramble and rescramble what I was doing in 1974, it is hard for me to recall why I was home at my parents', mid-morning on January 30th. I know this. My father had left for work. Kathy had left for school, ninth grade. I had left college after my sophomore year because I wasn't sure what I was doing, where I was heading, and it simply seemed economically wiser not to stay in school, taking what courses the whim struck, in search of and waiting for *the vision.* So I'd packed up and moved back to my parents' in June of 1973, had taken on sixty-three piano and guitar students a week, had started studying applied jazz theory for the piano with a guy from the Philadelphia School of Music, and had joined a band that played the usual firehouse-VFW-Elk Club-musty-roomed wedding receptions and Bar/Bas Mitzvahs. I had also rented a one-room with bath and closet kitchen in Media, Pennsylvania, a $99/month retreat, facilities and roaches included, on a back street I was sure no one in my family would happen to travel. It was sensible to retreat home till my career fog lifted, but it was equally sensible to invest some of my largesse in solitude, in sanctuary.

The house had once been a fine, large single-family home, perhaps a century before. It had an impressive main entrance, double wooden doors framed in stained glass, a chandelier high above an old and worn Persian carpet, but I mostly entered via the fire escape because of the neighbors on the first floor. Lou and Ellie were newly married, yet oddly lonely, it seemed to me — lonely, a phenomenon I could not understand then. And they were also a little weird. They liked to demonstrate the interactional closeness of their marriage by pretending they were saying exactly the same thing at the same time. Mind melding, sort of like coneheads, but embarrassing.

When I first moved in I was easy prey. The door to their apartment was right off the front hall. I would come in, never a quiet action what with the rasp of my key in the lock, the weight of the heavy double doors, the creaking of aged floorboards. I never made it past step three to the second floor. Lou and Ellie would burst out and then I was trapped. They would snare me with a pizza, a garbage pile, the works, from Pinocchio's. But the more we spent time together, the more they would entertain me by telling me things I was not interested in at all, and simultaneously at that. "Our mother, wife's side, is from Lancaster coming to visit." Or "We have third ticket to Dylan's concert. You come?" Somehow their mind-melding conversation required odd syntax and few articles. I wondered if they had rules like pig Latin rules. The very first time, I wondered if they were joking, but they were dead serious. I think if they had been joking, I could have accepted their routine. But they never for one moment did anything to let me believe it was a joke. Everything for them was serious, from a work-related spat over too many celery seeds in the coleslaw dressing (they ran a food truck restaurant at Drexel University) to Lou's devastation and fury when he went, uninvited, backstage to meet John Denver at a coffee house in Philly and Denver walked right by, ignoring Lou's outstretched hand. "Who does John Denver think he is?" they raged in unison, *accopiato*, Lou with tears in his eyes. What I would have asked, had I ever thought they were joking, was why Lou thought he could go backstage and accost John Denver in the first place? I finally began accessing sanctuary by stealing up the fire escape and going in a window that I always left unlocked.

I'd rented the apartment to have a place away from parents and Kathy and their adult/mid-adolescent turmoils. She was, at almost fourteen, well on her way to giving up on high school and rushing early into adulthood. Home was a battle zone, explosions unpredictable, but regular. I needed, at two weeks from twenty-one, more than the symbolic distance of a closed door. I needed real silence and solitude, something the Severn River had offered in bounty, something never present in the Pennsylvania world we inhabited, the one with new houses constructed of thin inner walls and close enough to neighbors that privacy was a fiction of politely averted eyes between satellite-dish ears. The only real secrets were those thoughts shared with no one, stored carefully behind blank faces. Now that I was old enough to try and achieve some semblance of a private life, I learned quickly how difficult and expensive it could be to recluse one's self successfully. Toward the end of my tenure in the efficiency above Lou and Ellie, they caught on to my use of the fire escape and window, even though I entered shoeless and after dark, never turned on lights, never played on the old trash guitar I kept stashed there. Even with no cooking, no flushing of the toilet until I was leaving, no conversing with the roaches — when I was there they would come knocking relentlessly.

Some people just never get even the most obvious clues.

I have always gotten over-peopled easily, too easily I guess, and what with all those piano and guitar students, K through 50s, and the seemingly endless weddings with the most unlikely guests asking us to do "Inna-Gadda-Da-Vida" or "Hey Jude" or "Pusher" just one more time one more time one more time now — I was having to deal with enough people in any given week to last me for any given decade. When one finds one's self purposefully singing "In da garbage da vomit baby" at someone's wedding reception, one must stop and take account. But that one-room in Media was no answer.

The last time I visited that apartment before finding another retreat, I didn't even go in. I sat in my car at the back of the alley parking lot behind the house and sipped on a quart of Pabst Blue Ribbon, thinking about a boyfriend who had told me that the last inch of any quart of beer was only the spit of those who were drinking it. I sipped for a bit, stopping several inches before that last inch, and after some contemplation of what and where next, I got out to pour most of the beer over the bottom step of the fire escape. A de-christening of sorts, a libation. Closure. Then I went home to my parents' home.

All this is context, reconstructing, to help me get at why was I at my parents' mid-morning on the 30th of January, 1974, when I probably should have been downtown in a psych or lit class at Temple University, still seeking that vision, but less expensively so. What I remember is coming into my mother's blue kitchen, headed somewhere in a hurry as always. She stood, leaning against the sill of the windows that looked out into our cul-de-sac of a backyard, where lawn and terraced flowerbeds that she had tirelessly crafted and divided evenly with slate steps were embraced on one end and the far side by a fifteen-foot curve of fieldstone wall. Above and beyond the wall was a deep woods, ours for a way, then belonging to a convent well on their other side.

My mother was crying. Silently but hard. And silent tears are the most devastating of all. They are not meant to be heard. They are raw anguish, pure grief, the epitome of our internal acid rains. Silent tears are the drowning sighs of all the sorrows one has chosen to keep within one's self lest those sighs, released, breathe hot scalding steam into the faces of those who look on.

How could I just go on and go wherever it was I had been going when my mother was dissolving before my eyes? I walked up behind her and leaned my head against her shoulder. No resonance. I wrapped my arms around her shoulders. She stood stiff, rigid, giving only one sharp shake of her head. I released her and she asked me to leave, not "get out" leave, but "go on as if I'd witnessed nothing" leave. I was tempted. Who would not have been? Coming upon sorrow of that depth is like coming upon a near-fatal accident with dreadful injuries that demand more than one has the knowledge to respond to. There was always the chance that I would come home later and all would be calm. But then there was always the chance that I would come home later and find a black gaping pit where home had been. I cannot say, now, what most made me stay.

The fear that if I turned my back the world would change inexorably was strong, paralyzing, but somehow I knew, too, that if I did not stay and try to understand my mother's sorrow, I would never understand anything of any importance at all for the rest of my days.

So she said, "Go on. I'll be fine. I am just being silly. We both have work to do," and I said "No. You are not fine. I can't leave until you are fine and there's nothing we have to do that cannot wait."

She asked with an edge of anger, "Can't you see I need to be alone?"

I asked back, tears in my own eyes, "Can't you see I can't leave you alone?"

And we held our places, neither giving the least sway. She cried through my silence, broken here and now with one of my unanswered unanswerable questions, attempts to get her to name exactly what was wrong, to pin it down so we could study it and fix it. Finally I stopped asking for those specifics. I had some premonition, perhaps, call it a reflex action, call it the subconscious or unconscious codependent response, call it love — I knew there were no answers and that I was there because of the fortune of time. My mother was suffering. She was, that day, fifty. She was at a loss. She was lost. Her life was passing before her eyes and disappointing her, partly because of things she had not done and partly because she could only see what she had failed at or failed to do she did not recall all the wonderful things she *had* done, the wonderful person she had always been. And partly because of things I will never know or understand. So I suddenly grasped one fact of life that I might never have understood had I not stayed that day — the greatest sorrows are unspeakable, unnameable. They cannot be pinned down and fixed or sent out for repairs. They can only be embraced and held, gently if possible, until they run short on energy and curl up for what one hopes will be a long and peaceful sleep.

The greatest sorrows, then, behave not unlike a child's tantrum. I mean this in no way to be reductive. While some may believe that tantrums are intentional and childish, I believe they are a very real last ditch effort to address some issue of great importance. When Kathy was a child, from ages three to six particularly, she fell prey to tantrums that could reduce any collection of adults to awful silence. She was inconsolable, blind with fury and distress, a tornado flailing to the rhythms of some inner demon. My grandmother and aunts accused her of *throwing* a tantrum, like one throws a spell. But her tantrums were too apocalyptic to have been within her power. We can be sucked into sorrow like lifeboats can be sucked into the vortex of their sinking mother ship. Sometimes I could only sit and watch Kathy, keep her confined, croon, hold her gently. In her teens, the tantrums ceased to be so overt, but they neither ceased nor lost their intensity and sincerity.

Imagine, then, such a tantrum in its most mature form, with all its physical torment internalized and invisible, the embodiment of mature misery. The gracious and considerate adult, and my mother has striven almost always to be naturally gracious and considerate, does not lie on the floor and scream or fling herself prostrate at the dining table and mar its good wood with trails of salty tears that will leave white spots. The gracious adult wraps her arms around herself and stands very still, very silent, her back to observers, her tears no more than dam overflow, her rage tightly leashed.

Thus stood my mother, gracious and contained while a

tempest wailed within her, and thus stood I, dimly understanding, my insides hollowing out as if to make some room should she need to share her tempest. As if outside myself, I could see us, the sixties formica kitchen table with its small gold fleur-de-lis between us, my mother leaning against the wall of windows, still but weeping, me standing five feet away unmoving, noting time passing by the hands of the clock on the stove, twenty minutes, thirty, forty-five, thinking that if we stood there all day and said nothing more, that would still be better for us both than my having left.

And then came the miracle, a subtle motion outside the windows at the top of the wall.

My mother and I must have felt that motion as one, looked up, as one, and hushedly expelled our breath, as one. Had there been angels gazing down on us we could have been no more greatly touched. At the top of the wall stood a thick herd of white tail deer, old and young, large and small, more deer than we could count, just standing there unalarmed, incautious, grazing on the stalks of dried summer flowers — purple cone flowers, African daisies, shastas, marigolds. We froze in place, as the deer would have had we come upon them, unexpected. We did not speak. Silently on our own we tried to count and to categorize so we could report this event with accuracy to my father and sister that evening. My mother and I began to breath again, in slow, quiet breaths, in and out, in and out, deeper and fuller, good air in, bad air out, renewing, detoxifying. There *would* be an evening, now, no doubt. We had real work to do. How many doe? How many yearlings? How many antlers on the largest buck? How many deer made up that peaceful brown blanket, splashed with the white of chests and switching tails, dewy with the many gentle ponds that are the eyes of deer?

Then, in a blur of slow motion, they were gone, taking with them all the sorrow in that kitchen and replacing it with awe. "Let's follow," my mother said. So we ran down to the mud space just inside the garage for boots and coats, gloves and hats, quietly eased up the garage door and quickly slipped up into the woods after the herd. We left the house unlocked. The danger had passed.

It was snowing? I had not noticed before. Small flakes, falling softly and slowly. As we tracked the deer into the woods, we were as silent as they because of that snow. At times, we would see them ahead of us, moving slowly, casually, out for a stroll, but not aimlessly. They clearly headed somewhere. When we felt too close we would stop and let them get ahead, leave us out of sight. After a while, though, we realized that there were deer moving parallel to us, at our pace, aware of us but unafraid, perhaps recognizing our scents from the iron salt blocks we put in the woods each fall. The woods was a contrast of browns and white. We moved slowly, perhaps two miles, to where the woods ended at the back of the Sabinases' furthest unused pasture. The deer stepped steadily forward, into the increasing pace of the snow. Some walked only twenty or thirty feet ahead, some closer than that — beside us, as if we had become part of their journey that day, if not part of their herd.

We moved into the wind skirting the farm's falling fences, up the hill toward where the convent perched, large and stark, a brown stone structure with small windows like a castle's, vertically rectangular and arched at the top. The convent also had its own graveyard, marked by carefully hedged yews. The entire convent grounds were set off by iron fencing, the sort with spikes. With the deer we walked the length of this fortressing and paused with them when the leaders of our herd stopped at Providence Road.

From the number of deer one sees dead on the sides of roads, one would think that deer did not think before they crossed human paths. Not true, or at least that day it seemed not true. Like crossing guards, some lead deer crossed and waited while some stayed behind to watch the others cross. This crossing place, a deep curve that was part of a long snaking stretch of Providence Road, arched in toward where we stood. Across the road was a steep rise rivered by many narrow deer trails. The curve, blind from any perspective, was so well-known as a deer crossing that yellow road signs alerted drivers for a half mile in both directions. The speed limit was fifteen miles per hour. Drivers obeyed. People told stories of cars and motorcycles hitting deer, the vehicles ruined, their passengers maimed or dead. We had seen deer crossing many times, had been prepared, always braking easily to watch them as we would a train or sheep or cows, even though deer pass mysteriously, wild and regal, reigning in the world but quick to take cover, to disappear. Crossing with them we became part of that mystery, magic, and no one saw, except perhaps some silent nun watching the snow from an upper window. Before any car came along, our herd had all moved out of sight, on across the Providence Road and up the many steep paths, to pick up an old rutted farm road, telltale only because of frozen fringes of field grass edging the uneven ruts, already softened by snow.

My mother and I lagged behind, just out of sight at the top of that rise. Our climb had left the palms of our gloves, the knees of our jeans, muddy and wet. We stood unprotected from the wind, at the top of a long wide field. Nothing human was visible — no house, not the road, not the convent. The deer moved out, a broad herd now, easily thirty in number. The farm road headed west across this expanse of field, and though we knew this area well, the geography had become foreign. We knew that behind us was the Sabinases' and the deer path to our house. We knew that to our left, a quarter mile, was a community of brick and wood houses. We knew that were we to follow the field parallel to the Providence Road, we would come to the juncture of Providence and Newtown. We could figure that this anonymous farm road angled down to the reservoir. But when one follows another's map, even that of a herd of deer, one enters a different country. So we stood for a bit, watching the deer move steadily away, wondering if we wanted to cross the border from our world into theirs. In a way I think we did not, but we continued, following them down the road until we were nearly caught up, until we could see the shimmer of the dark reservoir water, black through the haze of snow. We knew that they would continue on, circling back to the state park, following paths that people walked upon occasionally in bits and pieces, paths that the deer knew like people know their own highways. We knew that wherever they led us, we would be able to find our way back. So it was tempting to follow, to walk those paths in full circle with the deer, to know what few humans ever know, to walk as if with cloven hooves. But we also knew we were ready to go back and we did, following the same path, now returned to its normal identity as the woods path that runs from Ridley Creek Road through the woods behind our house and those of our neighbors, the path that moves between the fences of the Sabinases' small farm and the convent land till it ends at Providence Road. And as we returned, we made noise, released from our ghostly whitetail silence. All in all, we travelled about eight miles.

Did we talk about my mother's sorrow? I think we must have. I know that I need only say to her, "Remember your fiftieth birthday and the deer —" and she nods as if, for her too, it was just the other day. Knowing us as I do, I suspect my mother most likely first began to apologize for her show of emotions and that I, embarrassed, told her she had no reason to apologize. And she did not. Then I suspect she tried to explain and that her explanation shattered into bits and pieces, because what was unnameable that morning was no more nameable that late afternoon. I do remember her telling me what I had already glimpsed enough to begin learning that morning — that sometimes there is no rational explanation and there does not *need* to be: much that brings us sorrow is no more tangible than Emily Dickinson's "certain slant of light," and that many sorrows cannot be fixed, only endured and survived, and that some survivals are almost accidental, some almost miraculous, most only temporary. Gifts. Like crossing with deer at Providence Road. Like coming home from a journey no less fantastical than one from *The Hobbit* or *The Narnia Chronicles.* Our journey had in it, too, a resonance with earlier times, when a mother and daughter might have adopted the geography of deer because it was the only map that existed.

I remember emerging from the woods to find the evening

come and our house lit, my father and my sister, then fourteen, waiting to go out to celebrate my mother's fiftieth birthday, both worried some, but knowing my mother and I were with each other and could not have gone far. After all, we'd left the house unlocked. Our cars were both in the drive. We paused at the edge of the woods to practice our tale, to agree on how many deer, on how our journey began, how far we had walked. Little could we have explained in words, even to each other, that we had travelled into different lifetimes that day.

The World
When
We Are Not
In It

There's nothing like a new sibling to jolt a kid into an awareness of "other" — other than self, other than where self is, other
than what self is. Nan and Suz and I all got a new sibling the
same year, same month of our seventh year, March of 1960.
For all of us, these were our second siblings, and all of us were
in the middle with older sisters. I was the lucky one; mine was
a girl. Nan and Suz got boys. For me, the gender of our household remained in balance. For Nan and Suz, there was imbalance, subtle yes, imperceptible to adults definitely, but stated
in red neon as far as we were concerned. All of us had to deal
with the lifestyle shifts — feelings of displacement, babies take
time, hush you'll wake the baby, hush you'll wake your mother.
But when it's all one gender or the other, there's not that
tension of, well we didn't have sophisticated words for it, that
tension of *boys are better than girls.* Suz said that her dad, just
home from the hospital, had dialed the phone and without even

saying hello had just yelled to whoever answered, "It's a boy! It's a boy! It's a boy! It's a boy!" Over and again, as if whoever he called couldn't hear him the first time, she said. Nan said her father stopped calling her "my little girl" and had started calling her "Nan" and reminding her that she was getting to be a big girl. Now Nan had always hated the "my little girl" business, particularly when he called her that in public. "So what's my little girl been up to today?" he'd ask when we came home after some tricky negotiating of the swamp. Embarrassing, but to have him finally admit she was growing up just at the time when her brother was born, that had to be more than a coincidence. She was sad.

So though I was clearly the best off, we were still all pretty much in shock, and though we did not understand then what we can probably all name now, wherever we were, we became a support group, what the Chinese call a *talk bitterness group*. And bitterness we *did* talk, bitterness born of finding ourselves redefined without anyone asking our permission, bitterness born of adult ignorance, bitterness born of love/hate relationships with our new siblings. They were, after all, interesting and we felt a certain passion for them, particularly when no one was looking, but none of us was the doll-baby-can't-wait-to-be-a-mommy-gooey-gooey sort of girl. Our siblings were disruptive, they stank, and they spit on us. So while we had weak moments of succumbing to the fascination of minute finger nails and wrinkled palms and curled feet, surprising moments of gently rocking their carriages to put them to sleep, we hated those moments when an aunt or grandmother and even our mothers would sit us down, always in the middle of sofas, drape towels over our left shoulders and pin us down beneath those fragile fat little masses of spit and damp and stickiness. To this day, I loathe the scent of Johnson's Baby Powder and Johnson's Baby Oil. And to this day, I still slip back in time when a friend or niece sits me down and traps me beneath a baby. I feel residual panic. I recover quickly and the naturalness of them settles in, but then I was stuck in place till someone thought to take the baby off me.

We hated our siblings' infallible abilities to interrupt and take over any moment we were sharing with our parents and grandparents. We knew deep in our souls that we'd likely never be cute enough or smart enough to win our adults back, but beyond hurt and jealousy, beyond not knowing where to be, how to be, who to be — because now we were suddenly getting glimpses of our adults' perceptions of who we were, glimpses that conflicted with who we had been cruising along thinking we were — beyond all this, the three of us were suddenly awakened to the realization that while we were in school, life was going on at home without us. I don't know where we thought our mothers were before these births. It's not like we thought they had little switches and were turned off and stored in some closet like the robot Julie Newmar played in a TV show. But until this time, we had thought about our mothers solely in terms of us. Were they angry or happy with *us* when we left for school? Did they have plans for *us* when we got home from school? That is the privilege of the youngest except when an older sibling is going through some rite of passage — school proms, graduation from high schools, major dates, marriage. Our new siblings awoke us to the reality that our mothers were not just waiting for us to return from our days in school or at play as both they and we seemed to wait for our fathers. I remember one day coming home unheard to find my mother hanging sheets in a May breeze. It was a Saturday. My father's car was gone, my older sister nowhere in sight, my younger sister on a blanket on the soft spring grass, lying on her stomach straining up to watch her mother, my mother, who was clipping sheets to the long strands of clothesline, one side of a sheet to one strand, the other to the next, creating horseshoes of sheet, damp hammocks I had always wanted to lie in. She talked casually, nonstop to Kathy, regular talk, not baby talk. I could not make out her words, just her pitch and tone. I stood there with my bike and watched until she saw me, and suddenly I was back in the world.

But for the first time I understood quite profoundly that there were worlds happening when I was not around. I had had glimpses of that possibility before. There was clearly a world I was not in, for example, when I biked into Severna Park with empty bottles to trade in and came upon my father buying black walnut ice cream at the new High's store. There was another I was not in in moments when I crept upstairs to find my older sister humming with her radio while she painted at the small easel set up on the round table in her room. But the more I was aware of this phenomenon of worlds, the more I panicked when I thought of what I was missing and whether I was missed. Yet, more and more I withdrew to the shadows at the edges of others' worlds to observe and take stock, for all practical purposes invisible, perhaps even forgotten.

1962 It is lunch recess and I have slipped over the ridge that hides the railroad track and Severna Park from view and serves as a fence on the north side of our playground. A similar ridge hides Severna Park from the tracks. The space between the ridges is very quiet and deep, peaceful except when a train comes along. The sun is getting to that time of year when it begins to come down sharply, hot stalactites of air pricking the tops of heads.

I have slipped off the playground and out of sight because I am having a bad hair day. Sandra P. and her army of three have once again targeted me for their recess entertainment, surrounding me and accusing me of bleaching my hair. They have been making this accusation almost weekly all year, almost always on Mondays. I made the mistake one Monday of telling them that I wash my hair on Saturday nights and it just is lighter when I wash it. The day after this disclosure, Sandra P. came to school with a new word, "hygiene," and told me her mother said my mother should watch my hygiene. I ask her what "hygiene" means and she tells me "hygiene" means keeping clean. My cheeks go hot with burning blush, reddened shame. I bolt for the back of the playground, their laughter tinkling behind me, and when I get out of sight near the softball area, I scurry over the ridge and slide down the steep other side into the railroad bed.

My mother does watch my hygiene, but she and my father have begun handing responsibility for it increasingly over to me. I bathe regularly, but I only wash my hair when coerced. I hate washing my hair. The soap gets in my eyes. Water gets in my ears. The ubiquitous cup of cider vinegar, a final rinse, dribbles into the corners of my mouth sour and stinging. Rough towel drying pulls at my roots. And then the tangles. There is no such remedy, yet, as creme rinse or No More Tears. My grandmother would have me coerced more often. She has someone who "does" her hair, every once in awhile turning it blue. My mother and father tell her I am just going through a "phase" and it will pass. I am not so sure of that, but if believing so keeps them from making me wash it more often, I will not question their beliefs. I have been awarded the liberty of having my own bath, no help unless I ask for it, and asking for help with my hair would be to give up my liberty. By Saturdays, though, my mother and grandmother are insistent, saying my hair is greasy, the "s" like a "z" when my grandmother says it which makes the word sound far worse than it does when my mother says it. It is around this time that Peter the parakeet's vocabulary has expanded to include the word "dirty," and he seems naturally to pair it with Betsy. *Dirty Betsy.* I will never know who has taught him to taunt me this way. Perhaps his taunting just came naturally. Perhaps, sitting on my head or shoulder, my hair offended his aesthetic.

The long quiet trench where the railroad tracks run is a good place for contemplation. I walk for a while very slowly, searching the cinder ground around and between the rails. I balance for a while along one rail, its surface polished by steel against steel. I find a penny flattened to knife sharpness, perhaps one of mine. I often put pennies on the tracks in hopes of having one flattened out as evenly as one my father has — a thin penny, a perfect oval, elongated and concave. His has the Lord's prayer etched on the top of the arch. Lincoln's profile is elongated but easily recognizable on the underside of the arch.

I have been told not to play by the tracks and particularly not to put things on the tracks. During his boyhood, my father had a friend who liked to flatten objects on the tracks. Once he set out two large bolts, five or six inches long, three quarters of an inch in diameter, with large hexagonal heads. The boy could just imagine them flat and thin. When the train came, the bolts were too low down for the cattle guard to shove them, but they were tall enough to imbalance and topple the engine. No one was killed, but the engineer was hurt, a broken arm and some ribs. For a while, their town of Ellicott City was free of kids who put things on the tracks. The accident scared them all, and they all were told that much more damage would have been done had the train not been going slowly.

I have walked down the tracks until I am almost even with the school. I have ten minutes of recess left and so climb up the ridge and drop to my belly to slither forward in the tangle of morning glory vines and grasses. I want to get back unseen, but right below me on the new tarmac play area, the three teachers on recess duty stand tight together, the way we like them, paying attention to each other instead of us. They are talking seriously about something while all over the playground, my schoolmates play loudly. I can see one teacher, a third grade teacher, is crying. I wish I could hear what they were saying. I can tell by watching that the two teachers not crying are trying to soothe her, so the three of them are not having a fight. I slip back and away and go further down the track till I can slither up and over the ridge at the far end of the tarmac. No one sees.

I like and dislike finding myself outside of a world, watching it. I like and dislike invisibility. I feel powerful. I also feel sad, alone, uninvited, particularly when I can tell that no one noticed I was gone. That bad hair day, I stayed in the shadows of ridge and trees at the edge of the tarmac watching and waiting. If I had gone back to the open playground, Sandra P. and her friends would have started in on me again, and I was inept when it came to dealing with them. I was working hard to stop "initiating fights" on the playground. So I waited for the bell to ring and the three teachers to leave their conversation to gather us into lines.

During the late seventies and early eighties, I began having three recurring dreams of invisibility that surface even now, almost two decades later. In one, I sit on my desk in an office I share with seven fellow English Department teaching assistants and lecturers, an office under the stairs in the Carnegie Building on the Penn State Campus. In the office, sitting in a circle talking, are two women who will be lifetime friends, which of course I cannot know then. With them are their first husbands and my current boyfriend. My position on the desk is outside their circle, and as they talk, my contributions to the conversation go unacknowledged. Eventually, their conversation turns to focus on me, in third person, on what a downer I am to be around. In my dream, I beg *Hey! Hey! Just tell me what to do and I will change!* I get off the desk and walk between them into their circle. It is then I realize I am invisible. Well not exactly invisible, I have been rendered invisible to them until I learn how to be a better person. The dream goes on, though I recall it less vividly. I follow them to a restaurant, but am not allowed to eat. The waitress cannot see me. My friends know I am there, but they keep me invisible. One of my women friends relents a bit and orders an extra beer and says I can drink it, but nothing else, no food. I realize how much I am not in their lives both in the dream and out. The couples are soon moving on in their lives as couples and to distant new homes. The boyfriend is moving on in his life, to a summer job in the midwest, testing that world already in other women's beds before he leaves ours for good.

In another dream, I am the tender of a woman named Charlotte who has a bipolar problem. When she is depressed, she is a slender suicidal woman with black hair and full-length black dresses and fringed scarves whom I must watch very carefully. She seems to live alone, in an immense house with a formal garden full of trolls and gnomes that pop out when I take a break to go walking by myself and ask me, forcefully, over and over, "Who are you? Who are you?" I can never answer them beyond saying I am here to tend to Charlotte. Just that. There is family, all dressed formally in black and white, a brother and his wife, a sister and her husband. They appear sporadically, usually when I have nearly failed in my work keeping Charlotte from becoming manic, for it is then she turns into an orca, a killer whale, and then that I must paddle out on a blue surf board, hauling a bucket of raw meat with which to tempt her to shore, with which to beach her, at which point she will transform into Charlotte, slender and white paper pale, in a modest and plain black swim suit. Then I lead her back to the house and the cycle begins again. When I awaken from this dream, I write it down and then write it down the next time. It is always the same and I cannot unlock its message.

In the third dream, I am swollen with child, but I am also in pursuit of two villains. In a way, the dream is like a biathlon or some video game in which I must complete one level before going on to the next. The rule for this dream is that I must deliver six babies, by myself, each in a different setting. Between babies, I continue my pursuit of the villains, never any the less swollen with child until the end when, after delivering the last baby, on the altar in a abandoned church, I pursue the villains on a snowmobile through thick, almost liquid red mud until their emerald green 1952 Buick crashes into trees. Stunned, they are easy to apprehend and tie to trees while I retrace my journey to find the babies and call for backup. But I always wake before accomplishing either. The Buick is my mother's father's, the one he drove from new, the year before my birth, till sometime not long before his death in 1979.

Presence and absence are not simple opposites. Each can be the other. At all times the two conflate. Neither is predictably neutral or good or bad. Each instance defines the words for itself.

During the summers in Maryland, I did not go to church. My older sister went to church, to sing with the choir and to be, I believe, in a place where she felt very present and necessary. After Kathy came along, when a baby, she would stay with my grandmother. My parents and I would go to the river and swim and laugh and swim. I don't recall that Kathy ever came with us, though she was six before we moved to Pennsylvania. Perhaps my sister took her to Sunday School. Perhaps she simply went on staying with my grandparents for that hour or so. She was never an ardent swimmer.

The beach and the long pier were always empty those Sunday mornings and thus became magical, extraordinary. We played in the water like three children. My father would be a porpoise and I would climb on his back, arms wrapped around his neck, legs cinched about his waist, and he would dive and leap, and I would watch life beneath the water as he swam along the bottom, watch my mother swimming beside us, smiling. My mother and he would race, and she would always win. We would have water fights, with me on one or another pair of shoulders. I always ended toppling off and that was fine.

On those Sunday mornings, the beach and the river was a world only we knew. We were the only three people in it. The absence of all others was special, a gift. When the time came to go home where we joined with my sisters and readied for our mid-afternoon Sunday supper, I always felt I was returning from far away, from another country. I never wondered if my sisters, returning from wherever they had been, returned with their own sense of coming from a great distance back to the world. I think about those Sunday mornings, now, we were absent from each others' lives, and I wonder if my absence was as special to them as theirs was to me. It truly has faded from my memory whether either sister ever joined us.

I don't remember everything, but I do have that kind of way-back memory, the kind that people who don't have it deny exists. My first memories go back to when I was eighteen months, really, with no help from parents and pictures. I remember sitting on a screen porch, warmed by sun, cooled by gray painted concrete, and some plastic toy, yellow, blue, green, red, all sharp primary colors. I remember taking it apart and putting it back together. In my mind's eye, it was something like a boomerang. But what it was does not matter. It's the pleasure of the moment, the warm sun and cool concrete, the colors and the sense of my own dexterity.

I remember watching my father build a rail fence between

the front and back yards of our first house. I had developed a habit of wandering off. I watched him from the top rail of a finished portion. I was around two.

I remember my first lesson about electricity, my fingers touching both prongs of a plug before it was fully out of the socket. I remember lurching backwards and knocking a china lamp from a table and it shattering on the floor. I remember that my mother was not angry about the lamp.

I remember the morning I tired of my regular breakfast, a boiled egg with some bacon crumbled in it, taken with my father at the dining room table. I switched plates before he came to the table. I remember his look of surprise when he sat down to boiled egg and realized I was eating fried egg, over easy, on toast, a strip of bacon to the side. I remember that he and my mother laughed.

I remember a birthday cake shaped like a heart but made of ice cream instead of cake. Even though I could tell my parents thought of the cake as something special, I remember bursting into tears and not being able to stop. I remember that I felt bad that I could not stop. I did not understand the significance of a heart shaped cake for a Valentine's Day child. All I understood was that there was no cake, only ice cream.

All of these memories and the many more locked up with them are memories from my first three years. We moved from that first house to a larger one in June of 1956.

I remember the day my father's father died, October 16, 1956. I was three and he would have been fifty-three had he lived exactly two months more. December 16th. I remember him, in images yes, but clear images. Snapshots. Impressions. Scents and Sounds. Color. Mood.

In images I remember a man, old but not old, still with color in his hair. Reddish. I know that when we went to his and my grandmother's house, I mostly focused on him. I could jump up in the air high enough to kick my heels against my butt and then land on my feet. He loved this and I would jump and jump and kick butt, knowing that aside from my parents, there was no one else in the room who loved me so unconditionally.

My grandfather was dying the entire time I knew him and had started to do so six years before my birth, one year after his own last child was born. Cancer of the larynx. I remember that he spoke through something like a horn, a vibrating reed that my father tells me Bell Telephone built for him personally, the first person to experiment with a speaking device that Bell would later make with batteries. I did not know then that my grandfather was dying. The horn was just part of who he was, just as red hennaed hair and mink scarfs with mink heads, the mouths of which snapped on their own tails, were part of who the many adult women were who seemed always to be in my father's parents' house, The Crows' Nest it was called. I remember those mink scarves, one with three heads, women with hair impossibly red, sometimes with red scalps, my grandfather and his horn, a house never less than crowded, black Great Danes with six-inch strings of drool, loud sopranos screaming through an old radio on top of an upright piano in the front hall — Saturday's Metropolitan Opera, piped through wires and speakers which transformed what was no doubt exquisite into nothing but loud shrieks and frenetic unsettling noise. I remember too that someone in that house could not cook chicken without turning it to the texture of jerky.

October 16th, 1956, my family spent the day and evening at the Crow's Nest. The house was dark and abnormally quiet. My grandfather was not sitting in his usual chair, speaking through his horn and I did not know why, though someone no doubt told me something. The large rambling Victorian house *seemed* very empty. It may not have been. I was, I remember, very hushed. I remember actually deciding to go and find my grandfather and climbing unnoticed up the big front stairs to the second floor, consumed in darkness. After that I have two kinds of memory. Always there are my own flashes of memory, images made up of darkness then light, then darkness, of the heavy wooden straightback chair I sat on by the side of my grandfather's bed with its knobby bedspread. I remember sitting by that bed with my grandfather, knowing he wanted me with him. In my memories, he was there, lying in bed, his blue eyes open and looking into mine.

My second layer of memory of his death, a kind of memory that is shared and thus includes the interpretations of others, is from later, years later, after the death of my mother's mother, her heart shattering with the glass in her African violet window, after one too many arguments with my grandfather. She had been laid out in a funeral home, open casket. I commented that it was a shame she could not have been laid out in her own bed like my father's father had been, next to the old walnut desk where she often sat to write letters in her beautiful script on delicate stationery. My comment sparked my parents' memory of that night in 1956. They told me, then, about their search of the house when they noticed I was gone. Their search ended at my grandfather's room, where I sat on a chair that had been moved across the room and placed so I could sit facing the empty bed. (He was not laid out there, though to this day I see him lying there, animated, talking without his horn, leaning against his pillows in white flannel pajamas.) The chair was a heavy old chair I could not have possibly moved myself. The room was lit with lights I could not possibly have reached the switches for. And as my parents approached my grandfather's lighted room, they could hear me speaking as one does in conversation, talking some, quiet some, then responding to someone they could not hear.

Then my own memory, the flash image of their entry into the room, the scent of forced calm layered over fear. My parents told me those many years later that I talked all the way home, an hour's drive easily, leaning on the back of the front seat, telling them what my grandfather had said to me. I wish, like me, they had the habit of saving events, of writing them down for keeps. I wish any one of us could remember what I reported of my conversation with this man. Other than my three-year-old impressions of him, I have no idea what sort of person he was, what kind of man, except from stories I've been told over the years, but even in his long absence I have always felt the warmth of exchanged love.

Jayne Anne Phillips begins her novel, *Machine Dreams*, with a wonderful line. "It's strange what you don't forget." It is equally strange what you do forget, what you try to, what you refuse to. From somewhere else I recall this too: "I never know what to do with these goblins — they are the agents of human memory." It is true that memories have their own lives, that they are their own agents.

1994, November 21st, 10:23, evening   The phone is ringing when Neil and I unlock his back door. I have been waiting for one of *those* calls for some weeks. There unquestionably exists a sort of psychic anticipatory streak in my mother's mother's mother's side of the family. I've lived with it for too long to deny it, and

I know that my mother and hers, and her mother's sister, and my younger sister definitely have lived with it, too. And we have come to trust it, to respect it, but to like it is hard, impossible. Usually, the sense is quiet and gentle, though sometimes when catching me in a particularly dense mood, it calls me to attention harshly. People who don't believe in such perception kept me wary and cynical about mine well into my early adult years, but the fact is, I have felt stuff coming for as long as I can remember, and several times in my life I have connected somehow with the newly dead as they passed on to wherever. And sometimes, I have not connected where it would seem I should have: I had no warning of my grandmother's death, did not feel her heart break, did not know what to do with her death when the news of it was passed on to me. Perhaps we did not have the right connection. When my grandmother's sister died in a Baltimore hospital around three in the morning near the very end of December, 1979, I awoke from a dream where I slept in a guest room in Elysian Fields in New Orleans. I dreamed that my mother called to tell me that someone had died, but the connection was bad and I couldn't hear who. After several attempts to hear her better, the connection broke. I awoke scared, crawled from my twin bed across that of the friend I was travelling with. She awoke as I knocked her crawling past and together we searched quietly for a watch while I told her my dream. We found the watch at a few minutes after three. Late the next afternoon, tired of my obvious uneasiness, Erika said, "Call home, Liz. Then you will know." So I did. It has been reassuring to have had a witness to this passing of my Great Aunt Lee, who had in some ways terrorized me as a child simply because she was strong and imperative, but she lived in what she called her "witch's house," raised cats and knew her herbs, goals I aspired to from early on in my life. I knew, very early on, that there was some part of her in me, and while the same is, I think, true of my grandmother, the connections I feel with her have been long in making themselves known.

The sensing in itself is not frightening, but as I have grown to believe in it, I pass into a sort of resignation and depression when it begins. I never know specifically who or what, just *that*, so there is nothing I can do, though I always worry that I could have done something had I been more open.

As we grew older and more open about whatever this sensing is, my mother and Kathy and I talked when we start feeling something. We sent out alerts. We checked on each other and others. We give cautions — take care, don't do this, do that. In late October when I last spoke to my younger sister, finalizing plans for a Thanksgiving gathering of her family and our older sister's family to celebrate our parents' 50th wedding anniversary, my sister and I got into lecturing each other, as we always have. I asked after her weight and told her to lose, that she was getting too old, almost thirty-five, to be so overweight. She got pissed. I said, "I just want you around for a long time." We spoke words of love, then, and I thank God for that because it turns out that this time, she *was* the phone call I was waiting for. I would be shattered now if we had parted in anger. That sounds cliché, but it would have been so easy to have waited a day or so too long to make up, to have waited till she was here with me, celebrating our parents' anniversary. Even though that final parting in anger would have been an accident, not reflecting our relationship at all, that anger would have been something I would have always had with me to mark her death, like a picture of me with four parrots on my shoulders and the witty card I saved to give her when she came. Like the Christmas present I brought her back from Paris, a compact with a cover on which some craftsperson has depicted, with bits of flowers from Provence, a night scene with flowering trees and a quarter moon. She will never see and study her face in this mirror that I almost sent her for her thirty-fourth birthday, but at the last minute held back for Christmas. There are so many errors we can make when we forget about death.

I remember the 21st quite clearly. I begin the day in a spat with Neil because he observes that I've been putting off, till the last minute, the complete planning and purchasing of the celebratory weekend's food. My first appointment is with a student with whom I have had the same conversation at least nine times before. We come to resolution, but only for a week before he is back, same question, same confusion. The day goes on long, and twice I think of calling my sister. She has been on my mind since that last phone call. Instead, I start switching back and forth between plans and lists for the weekend, responding to students' essays, meeting my classes. Finally, I join Neil for an evening at the symphony. But as we drive towards the music hall, Carpenter Center, I feel the tightness of panic in my chest. The student essays wait patiently in my briefcase, the ones that I have promised to have in a certain place for students to pick up by one the next day, the 22nd. I have all the next morning to finish. There are only eight, not that many, but I cannot stop the panic. By the time we park and begin our walk to the center, I am explaining, insisting, adamant that he go into the music while I sit in the lounge on the second floor and finish with the essays.

During the intermission, he brings me some champagne. The room fills with smokers. I find myself hardly able to breath, but I am all spread out at a table and, really, the intermission is always short. When all return to the music, I open a window and the smoke fades. My ability to take in deep cleansing breaths returns. But how sad I feel, hollow, weepy. I leave the essays to get another glass of champagne before the symphony bar shuts down. Fifteen minutes into the second half of the concert, I finish with my students and put things away and and *and* then the emptiness is all I have to focus on. I sit very still. I wait. The concert ends. Neil retrieves me. We drive back to his house, me trying to explain what I cannot explain, why it was that I had, simply *had* to get those essays done. And when we finally get to his door, the phone is ringing and he answers and again I wait, very still, almost serene, knowing the call is for me and knowing it is bad even before he turns and says, "It is your mother and it is bad news," and I ask "Is it my father?" and he says, "No, it is your sister," and I gasp my older sister's name and he says, "No," and after a pause, "It's Kathy" and I step away and say very clearly, for logic's sake, "No. It cannot be Kathy. How can it be Kathy? She's only thirty-four," and he's holding out the phone to me and I take it and try to make my voice sound normal and it is my mother and it *is* Kathy and she is dead dead how can she be dead she is only thirty-four and how can she be oh my God and I crack and my throat fills with gasps and sobs and I say "I'll be right home," and my mother says "No, stay there," and I say "No I will come home. I must," and I hang up and cannot breathe. The gasps and sobs fight each other for exit and I feel wild, feral, and vicious I want to smash smash anything, to sweep, with a long arm the surfaces of tables clean and and yet my feet are rooted by Neil's kittens which curl around my feet in distress and Neil presses a glass of something to my lips, not understanding that if I try to swallow against the gasps and sobs that I will die, that I may be dying, that my baby sister has died and that I just cannot accept that, that I never will.

We drive back to my house. Only my wrestling with the tangle of gasps and sobs breaks the silence.

Seneca says of asthma that physicians have called it a rehearsal of death, "since sooner or later the breath does what it has been trying to do all those times." When Neil gets me back home, I find myself almost shy as I enter the front hall and my parents, weeping, converge on me and we huddle. There is nothing to say. I go to my part of the house and call my brother-in-law and let him talk and describe to me the scene he will describe to me over and over for the next five days, until I can see it and feel it so sharply that I was there and mine were the arms into which my sister fell when she fell back blue in the face, eyes open, her soul passing as the ambulance arrived just too late to revive her. "People do not look the same when they are dead," my brother-in-law will tell me evening after evening as, we sit at his dining room table trying to make sense, trying to accept, trying not to completely lose it in front of the younger two children who are grieving in ways we cannot understand. "I made them let me see her and it wasn't her anymore." He will tell me all this while we wait in some alogical lacuna for the phone call from the hospital that will tell us that a mistake was made, a terrible wonderful mistake, that patients got confused and our Kathy is alive and fine and coming home. He will continue to tell me after we have passed back, if only momentarily, into logic and said to each other that "We have to believe this. She is dead. We have to believe."

On the drive north the next morning, my parents and I float between silence and meaningless small talk and wracking sobs and memories and rationales and fury. There is a point at which my parents talk on and on about which rivers in this region flood the most and the worst. They talk on and on. I manage to hold inside the yell that pushes against my larynx. I want to yell and say, "For God's sake shut up shut up! Who gives a good God damn about flooding rivers. Kathy is dead." But I know, the good me knows that they need to talk like this, to take breaks from silence and talk of grief. So I drive like fury. I don't care if a cop stops me. I almost want a cop to stop me.

I have cried so much since the phone rang that I can hardly see. I should not be driving, but better me than my parents. They quake visibly. We make a four-hour drive in three and five minutes, even with one stop to buy gallons of fresh fall cider. Kath loves good cider. We are thirsty, but instead of drinking some cider before starting off again, we store it safe and upright in the car and I hit the gas. I make no wrong turns and barely slow down for small towns. We plunge across the bridge at Point of Rocks, pass Frederick, and climb up into the Catoctin Mountains of western Maryland. I am going nearly eighty and am nearly blinded by the mucous of grieving eyes. I dare a cop to stop me. I want to be stopped by some calloused stranger who will try to fine me for charging to my sister's house, to my dead sister's children and husband. We cross into Pennsylvania and I am soon flinging us around curves on the final back roads. We have driven on these roads so many times. I drive them today and feel I have never seen them before.

New Oxford, PA, November 22, 1994

Dear Kathy — I am going to miss you so incredibly badly. You've been my little sister forever. You've been my friend almost as long. When the phone rang last night and Neil said, "It's your mother and it's not good news," I knew it was you. I cannot process the fact that you are gone forever. I am sitting at your dining room table with your beautiful daughter. We are writing in our journals. We are missing you. We do so differently. Sarah seems practical, but I distrust it. She refuses to get into any discussion which will make her lose her composure. She's a lot like you in that respect, though I hope, like you, she finds the freedom of owning openly all she feels.

Dave is in really bad shape and we — Mom, Dad, and I — are at a loss as to how to help him or the kids or ourselves. We are here and willing, but the fact is, everything is in place except you and nothing we can do can return you.

It's later now and now Dave is sitting here with Sarah and me. Al and Jesse have run away from the house. None of the kids is crying. I cry. Dave cries. He is supposed to provide the minister with things to say about you and somehow he has gotten the impression that he has to come up with upbeat material. He has wonderful memories, but no matter how upbeat those times were, all now is an emblem of loss. He needs to feel his pain. It is so very deep. It will never go away. Right now, each time the phone rings, he grabs it hoping it is the hospital calling to say a mistake has been made, that you are alive and someone else is dead. Each time it is not the hospital, you die again for him. For me too. I share his hopeless hope. I have told him to write you a letter, to write what he is feeling and forget the minister. This is no comedy show we are preparing for. It's a terrible goodbye.

All the way up the road today, I was so angry at myself. I've been so obsessed with my work, with getting tenure, that I've not seen you enough the last few years. But what is enough? I guess when someone you love dies, there never could have been enough.

Your children are beautiful. Jesse is tall and handsome, even with his temporarily maroon hair. Alex is sprouting and so full of energy that we are making him walk your Danes. Sarah is mature and honest. I love them and I look in their faces and see you. I will do my best for them, but God, I wish you were here. I expected we'd get old together.

I look around this home and see you too — your art, your treasures, your creation of a home with very little but love with which to create. I know you have not always been full of joy, but I know that you have been fuller and fuller as each year has passed. I only wish you had lived to become fuller still.

Today, people have been coming by endlessly. The ice box is full of food. The kids are eating — somewhat compulsively I must say. Dave eats nothing. Your dogs and cats are looking for you. They hear you in my voice, but I am not you.

David has told me the story of your death. Over and over. So vivid. I know it is imprinted and that you will die for me many times, and so painfully. Why didn't you go get the Proventil? If you'd had it, you would be here now, getting ready to come to Richmond. Why weren't you open about how bad you were feeling, about how bad the asthma was? And was it even asthma? All our lives you have been so frivolous with your health. Why? Look what you have left behind. Yes, I'm angry with you. You must have been angry yourself in those last moments, so frightened and angry. I am going to go read to Sarah now. Good night. Love you most always — Bets

Who is going to call me Bets now that you are dead? Damn it, Kathy.

Kathy has been dead for two weeks and three days. A friend has told me that I must start adjusting. She does not mean not to understand. I'm not really convinced that she doesn't. But if so, I don't think I can ever adjust. What is a sister but part of you? Her voice and my voice were so much the same on the phone that people calling to express their grief had to relive her death in a small way as I have been reliving it in larger ways, several times a day. When I call her house and her daughter answers, she mistakes me for her mother and is terrified. Part of me is dead. Part of me is no longer in the world.

It is noon on Sunday, January 15th, January 1995. Since 2:30 P.M. on Thursday, I have slept solid sleep for a sum total close to forty hours and will log another fifteen to twenty before spring semester classes get underway on Tuesday. I have finally listened to myself — my body, its cravings, my voice, its tonal messages. I have begun writing out my anger and seeing how to come to terms with it and with the fact that there are very few things I can do about it, that I will only do harm to myself and others to articulate it, and that I should learn from it and then *let it go*. But now I question myself — have I really counselled myself? In a way, it feels that I did, but there was a day and night, this Friday and Friday night, when I felt my sister Kathy constantly and tangibly.

Friday morning, I awoke in tears from a dream of her. I wept to school and, oddly, it was a day when people kept coming up to me and saying "I am sorry for your loss." *Your loss*. Your *loss*. I have heard those words so much recently that I just want someone to say it straight — "God, what an incredibly terrible thing. Your sister died. Are you okay?" I know people have meant well, but I wonder why it is we cannot call the dead *dead*. My little sister is dead at age thirty-four and I could not be any more unhappy, ever, than I have been since that call came. These people, I know are well-meaning, being careful, but their choice of "loss" did not keep me from breaking down and crying in public several times. And when several apologized for embarrassing me by making me cry in public, I realized that I was not embarrassed and said so and apologized for embarrassing them, if I had. I am not embarrassed to cry about my sister's death.

But this Friday, all day, I could not get Kathy out of my head — her voice, her infectious laugh, her wheeze that I have so long taken for granted. I wanted to call her home and see if she answered. And yes, I am well aware of the multiple levels of meaning in this last sentence.

When I went home Friday afternoon, I had a note from a niece, my older sister's middle child, thanking me for some earrings I'd sent her for Christmas. In it she wrote, "Please don't get me anything for my birthday. Just put what you would spend on me in the trust fund you are setting up for Kathy's kids." That evening, at a gallery opening down town, I bought my niece two ceramic candlestick holders and this weekend four lovely candles to use with them. After the gallery opening, I went to a folk concert. I was still tired, and I resisted going, but Neil insisted, ignored my hints, my whining, and by the end of the concert, for some reason I was feeling joyful, almost explosively so. That night I dreamed about Kathy again, and in that dream she said, "Holly will love those candlestick holders." I asked, "How do you *know* that?" She said, "I know. That's what counts. Do you know why you bought them?" And that was when I heard what I will write my niece when I send them. I will write her and say "Don't start off in your early adult life giving in to a woman's habit of denying herself for others. If you want to toss a five into the trust fund here or there, fine, but it's your birthday, and I love you and love getting you presents."

Last night I dreamed I was amongst people. Acquaintances and strangers, friends and enemies, family, even my parents. In this dream I wore only a pair of jeans — no shirt, no bra — and I was not spectacularly svelte. But I felt free and unembarrassed and sad for those who thought I should put on a shirt and feel otherwise. Today I awoke to what seems a new world.

Neil, unlike his neighbors and most of America, has not bothered to fight nature to create lawn. The community he lives in was once a wild deciduous forest, blanketed by leaves, patched with elegant little evergreen carpets of pipsissewa, a haven for arboreal birds and tree frogs. This morning, I awoke very late — 9:30 — to a ceiling that was tinted with pink. At first I thought something was making the painting on the wall opposite the bed reflect its pink upward, but there was no logical explanation. Then I realized that the pink was coming in through the window, that the night's rain had soaked the thick layer of ruddy, russet leaves on the ground outside, that the clear light filtering through tall leafless oaks and hickories was drawing pink light up from the leaves on the ground, and through some refraction of light and water and color, recasting the bedroom ceiling in pink. A glowing pale pink. I felt honored to see this phenomenon and honored to know what it was, to understand how it came to be.

A luminescence of leaves.

What
the River
Means

In the first half of the 1600s, during the British Civil War, ten Puritan families, Roundheads, came up from Virginia to Maryland where religious diversity was more tolerated. They established Providence, the original settlement on the Severn River. In 1650 Providence was "erected" into a county named after the wife of Cecil Calvert, Lord Baltimore, the Lady Anne Arundel. The county name, Annarundell, changed to Providence when the Puritans gained power in 1664, but only for two years before Anne Arundel once again had a county as her namesake. Annapolis was originally Anne Arundel Town, a small town but one of the new country's most important because of its extensive population of impressive lawyers, Francis Scott Key and William Pinkney to name two, and because it was the site of one of the country's earliest colleges, St. John's College, chartered in 1784 and opened in the fall of 1789. From early settlement on, the Chesapeake never went untouched by the many wars England involved herself in, but the Severn, unlike some of its sister rivers, remained mostly uninvolved, perhaps because it led to no important harbors, perhaps because its banks gave no rapid access to cities. Its primary role has been to provide homes and spawning and nesting grounds for the rich web of plant and animal life. The river has long been a sanctuary, an estuary yawning wide into the Chesapeake where Annapolis reigns and the waters are salt.

At the river's source the waters are fresh and narrow and called the Severn Run. There, some anglers tie their own flies and fish for bass and trout. When I was a child at the river's mouth, we fished for blues and trolled out into the bay over oyster beds for rockfish. Throughout the river's length, between Sandy Point where the river turned sharply right and the first bridge down toward Annapolis, we fished for white perch and yellow perch, the latter my favorite fish and perhaps the most beautiful in the river. Yellow perch, like tigers, shimmer and glow yellow gold through black stripes, narrowing as they move from back to belly. Spinous dorsal fins can flare like those of sailfish. A girl can really gore her palm on a yellow perch's fin.

Sometimes, on the back coves, when my parents' freezer was stocked with eating fish for the winter, my grandfather and I would chum with canned corn for carp. Carp, by my extended family's tastes, were inedible, heavy, oily. Just large goldfish. When the first enclosed mall was built near Glen Burnie, my grandmother never failed to comment that the large orange and speckled fish in the fountain pools were "nothing but carp."

My grandfather liked to catch them for the sport. Carp were, to me at least, immense, three feet long often and very heavy. They fought and twisted and, frankly, I hated fishing on carp days. I don't think I have ever enjoyed fishing for the kind of conquest that makes fishing a sport. I fished for reasons one might label as survivalist, though that word is too dramatic. I fished for pride. I fished to contribute to my immediate family. I felt, though I do not know if it was true, that the fish I caught lowered our food bills. All summer I would fish and clean, and we'd freeze the fish in meals for five, in blocks of ice. My family ate fish all year with regularity. My grandfather did not eat fish at all. Fish had made him sick once as I remember, and from then on he never ate them.

When he and I fished for carp we'd always throw them back, a little sore about the mouth but well-fed on the corn we chummed. I never thought about chumming when I was fishing. It was just a thing we did. For other fish, we chummed with other bait. We chummed for blues with crushed soft-shell clams, a delicacy in Boston, but considered inedible in Maryland when I grew up. We'd chum with chicken entrails and cornmeal, but for what I forget. Chumming, which transformed the water around our boat into an all-you-can-eat buffet, seemed a natural part of fishing, while crabbing at night with a strong flashlight was entrapment, unethical and a legally punishable deed. I did not think about the fairness of chumming then, but I think of all that chumming now, its logic and its ethics. A person casts temptations overboard — softshell clams, slightly crushed but still in the shell, corn from a can, a toadfish slain and quickly filletted, strips of smelt and other bloody bits and pieces — and then the person waits, with baited hooks swaying in the water, till a feeding frenzy develops, the sin of gluttony invoked by the ladling out of temptation.

The fish were rarely visible at first. Then the water grew

agitated, miniature white caps and cross currents, and finally some unlucky fish nabbed those suspended bits of chum with the surprise centers. Hooked, fish came aboard, were de-hooked and secured. Then we'd bait and cast again. If keepers, the fish went on the stringer with their peers or into the cooler or into the offerings bucket if they themselves might become chum for their chums. I remember wondering if fish had families, if those caught and waiting on our stringers in the home waters they would soon leave were visited by their spouses and children who came to see what they could do, and able to do nothing, to say goodbye.

The river was and remains a place of recreation as well as a place of business, though I imagine that increasingly any business now has been spawned by varieties of recreation. Last year, from a glance through the yellow pages in a Baltimore hotel in Harbor Place, I was able to trace more quite a few childhood acquaintances who supply food, skis, guidance, river-related equipment, rentals, lessons, and boats. A woman who went to school with my older sister saw the trend and moved south to be a rental property entrepreneur at a beach resort. But in my time recreation was relatively simple, boats of most genres, some fast, perhaps dragging skiers, some more in tune with the rhythms of the river and its surroundings, moving only with the wind. Sailing can be a formal or informal avocation, the skipper's and crew's merit decided by how well each knew the names of ropes and knots and all the parts of different sailing crafts, decided too by how strongly they eschewed the use of motors for any nautical purpose other than moving a large sailing craft through Kent Narrows with its drawbridge or some similar stretch of water where windpower would be too much of a risk.

I was an informal sailor, sometimes sailing in our canoe until the day its aluminum mast bent right at its middle, ninety degrees, when the canoe capsized and rammed its mast into a sandbar. We had, for a while during my older sister's teens, a real sailboat with a pedigree, a Racing Hampton, which my parents and sister sailed with some ease while I huddled out of their way and the way of the boom, cold and inept. And then, of course, there was the Sailfish, red with gold and silver and black sparkles, a simple slice of fiberglass that I threw around the summer river with abandon when I was thirteen and madly in love, sitting in its minimal indentation for its lone passenger. Alone, I sailed from love into its aftermath, sailing from dream back to reality, recognizing that my love never had done more than talk about the Model A or T he was rebuilding and play board games with his nephew and me or tag along when his nephew and I went swimming or walking. Sailing can be an a formal or informal avocation, but it always is a site of meditation.

Water decks, those motorized rafts with awnings and fence-like sides, those were my secret favorites, though we never had one, and my sole experience on one was one Fourth of July when a new neighbor in one of the many houses leaping up on the peninsula invited my parents to join them. My younger sister and I went along, my older sister off with friends. The next year, no children over five were invited, for reasons we could never know, though I suspect it was because I made their deck more like a boat by diving off and jiggling their drinks as I climbed back aboard, dripping with abandon as fireworks soared overhead in great splashes of colored stars. I liked those raft boats because they had no demands associated with them. I think they gave me my first definition of leisure, time without some mission, adults sitting in lounge chairs under an awning with the lull of the water luring them to linger a bit longer than they might in their own back yards: aimless cruising, the water version of the Sunday drive, following one's whims, moving gently off shore, meandering into coves, with a picnic lunch of fried chicken and potato salad, devilled eggs, stalks of celery, carrots, black olives and sweet pickles. A gallon thermos of iced tea or lemonade. A tub of ice, cans and bottles, always with a church key hanging from it to open the cans of beer and bottles of Frosty Root Beer and Orange Crush.

Fishing and crabbing were less attractive to some recreationists than boating of whatever style, but fishing and crabbing were always options. How often one pursued these creatures, as well as the manner in which one did so and what one did with any catch, distinguished business from recreation. The recreational waterperson rarely went out during the prime biting times, early early morning or dusk. The recreational waterperson sometimes threw back any catch rather than clean or cook it and, when fishing, rarely had any comprehensive agenda as to what to catch. My grandfather and I always went out for a specific fish, always somehow knew where to go, and always had a good idea of how many we could catch and needed to catch, determined by the taste buds, the season, the number of mouths to plan for around the table or the particular use to be made of the catch.

I imagine that now the definition of recreation has expanded and redefined the business of the river significantly. I doubt there is an old dark tavern near Severna Park that will buy crabs by the dozen from an eleven-year-old girl. I doubt there is a grocer who will buy her homegrown muskmelons. I know the day has passed in many states when kids make good money off returnable bottles they cull from roadsides, and shores and bushes along the railroad tracks, natural acts of recycling, no signs announcing that this or that groups has adopted a roadside and is keeping Maryland beautiful. I imagine, though, that there's still money to be made by the industrious child following An Event — such as the annual Indian Landing Regatta, the Beach Flea and Antique sales, and the Oyster Roast (misnomer, for while there always was a steamship roast to carve on, most oysters were swilled raw at this event, delicately decanted from their sharp shells into raised mouths, tongues ready, oysters raw and gelatinous from their half shells, perhaps seasoned first with red sauce, horseradish or lemon).

After An Event, I was as accurate as any mechanical metal detector. I would get up at dawn, forego the crabbing, and head for the beach to begin a systematic scanning of every inch. One-by-one, a few other hunters and gatherers would join me, and like some herd of peculiar animal, we'd stalk the lost penny, dime or quarter. Our heads bent at the same angle, we would take a step and scan, take another step and scan. I got very good at finding coins and keys and jewelry without even trying, the correct shimmer snagging the corner of my eye and stopping me in my tracks. To this day I find money daily and sweep down to pluck it off the ground and garner wishes. But then I stashed it in my old plaster pig bank, large enough to hold a gallon and a half, old enough to have needed repainting and gluing several times. A second year birthday present, I believe, the pig was broken severely several times during its life, and I remember the day I found it broken beyond repair, several years after we moved to Pennsylvania, by a guest at a tenth grade party in search of petty cash who took more than he probably knew when he took my stash of Franklin fifty cent pieces.

By the mid-sixties, pollution threatened the river's health and that of all who swam within it. Yet before that human-made pollution, I remember an earlier year when the red tide devastated the river and the rhythms of my summer. In biological terms, the red tide is a vast conference of microscopic dinoflagelattes which secrete a powerful neurotoxin that accumulates in the tissues of shellfish, making them poisonous to predators; but I remember the explanation for the red shimmer of the river as a coating of algae that kept oxygen from water life, effectively smothering that life, leaving schools of fish and armies of crabs dead, washed up on the shore. The red tide is nature's pollution, unpredictable and no doubt with some natural purpose. But the old appliances and tires from people too lazy to find the proper dumps, the sewer runoff and waste oil, the gasoline from boats, the fertilizers and lawncare toxins from the manicuring of golf courses and rich people's grounds — these altered the river's natural chemistry in dismal ways, too. Some water life has no doubt died out completely. I reckon the number and kind of frogs have dropped starkly. Frogs, like lichen and most mosses, cannot stand much invasion of their fragile ecosystems.

Toward the end of our life there, I could not swim without developing large scaly patches that at times were red and at times ran clear fluids. When I was young in the river, opening my eyes under water was more comfortable than opening them in fresh air. I imagine the ph was balanced and the salinity a perfect match for my own. I could see, when in the water, peer down through it to the bottom at five feet, unless the weather had been rough and stirred up the water's natural sediments. By the time we moved away, I had spent a summer unable to swim because of scales and burning eyes. In a sense, when we left, it was time for us go. It would have broken all our hearts to watch the river as we'd known it die. I knew this then, even though I felt ripped raw, full of a degree of anger I had never known, vengeful and bitter, most likely bolstered by fear of the very different world I was cast into, one inexorably modern, invasive, adolescent, and limited in its boundaries. While the river had given me instincts, concepts, for when to stop, there had never been any rules beyond staying off the cliffs and getting home in time for dinner. I stopped my outward travels at natural boundaries or for natural reasons — the tide turning, the light failing, the surface roughening, the sun scorching, the gut knowledge that I had gone as far as I physically could and still get back in time. Beyond that, there had been no boundaries, no limits.

The first few years we were in Pennsylvania I went back fairly often to visit my mother's parents and my older sister, by then herself a mother, and also to visit my group of friends. But even those returns became tainted by the simple fact that my absence decreased in importance. More and more I was a visitor, a time warp, inadvertently invasive. I saw a life I had been part of going on without me, and finally I let it go.

The last time I visited, I went to a dance with these friends, the last time I would see all but one of them. I was sixteen. I slow danced with the brother of my erstwhile best friend's boyfriend. The nuns censoring such behavior tapped us to move further apart, several times, as they did most every other couple on the floor. I do not remember much of that evening until I returned to my grandparents' and let myself in. I crept towards my grandfather's den where I was sleeping on a day bed. Moving through the dining room, no lights, I knocked a chair just before I went through the door into the back hall.

My grandparents had had separate rooms as long as I had known them. He slept at one end of the hall in a bed specially built to accommodate his height. My grandmother slept at the other end of the hall, unrocked by the wake of my grandfather's weight as he moved in his sleep. This night, as I passed across the hall that ran between their rooms, I heard two metallic clicks, almost simultaneous, and instincts dropped me to the hall floor. I had grown up around guns and recognized their subtle sounds. From the floor I called, "It's Betsy. Betsy." No one spoke back, but I heard the snap of hammers' return and I heard the bedside table drawers open. I heard each receive something solid and hard, and close as I completed my crossing and shut the den door, my heart beating too fast, my insides hollowed out and collapsing.

I had driven myself down and suddenly felt desperate to slip out and drive north and home. But that rudeness my grandparents would never have understood, much less forgiven, even if they recalled the night before. So I sat and stared at the black rotary phone on my grandfather's desk and thought of calling home. But the fear and anger that would instill in my mother and father would have been an act of cruelty, for what could they do? I finally slept, in my clothes and shoes, and changed the next day into jeans for the drive home. With my grandparents I sat down to a breakfast of boiled eggs with butter on toast with bacon. They asked only if I had had a good time and who I had danced with and enjoyed my stories. My grandfather winked a lot when I told them about the nuns maximizing the distance between the couples dancing. My grandmother mentioned that she'd heard some talk that the boy I had danced most with had been in trouble. I told her I couldn't imagine. Neither mentioned their catching me in their cross-hairs, something I suspect they'd welded into their dreams or forgotten.

I cannot seem to make myself go back there now.

When I drive from Richmond to Baltimore, the temptation grows intense, every time I approach exits to Annapolis, to turn off to the right at Benfield Road — Benfield Boulevard now — and to drive down a road once bordered by tall pines and deciduous trees and later by occasional houses which even later merged into communities with names, like Chartwell and Severn Estates. Following Benfield Road, I would eventually pass St. Martins-in-the-Field Episcopal Church, where my older sister married in 1966, where I went to kindergarten and learned about having one's mouth washed out with soap, where Father Heck was the pastor most of my life there, retiring his pastorship to Father Libby who took up Heck's mission in time to marry my sister and her fiance. Soon after, Father Libby moved across the river to St. Stephen's Church in Severn Parish, and in 1967, I stood up in that church, which I remember as dank and stone, but exquisite, as sponsor for my sister, Kathy, then seven, and as godmother to my first niece, then less than two months old, as they were baptized, on that June day, with my mother's mother, born in 1895. Grandmother, granddaughter, great granddaughter.

If I turned right onto Benfield Boulevard now and continued past St. Martin's, I would pass, further on on the left, the Severna Park High School, my sister's alma mater. Every Halloween the high school students made money by throwing a fair, complete with a Ferris wheel and many booths. But most important was their transformation of the vast maze of school basement into a haunted place. One Halloween, as a friend of mine, Maggie, and I threw pennies at small fish bowls, her younger sister was hit by a car because she had, for some reason, decided to strike out for home. Perhaps she was bored. Perhaps she thought we had lost her and she was scared. But already the growth was upon Severna Park and the boulevard that ran perpendicular from Benfield Road, along the front of the high school, was two lanes both ways. None of us were schooled in crossing such a road. Crossing was forbidden to young kids unless a responsible person was attending. Maggie and I, for the first time in our lives deemed responsible people, responsible enough to mind her, each holding a prize goldfish in a plastic bag of water, looked for the sister for quite a while, noting the commotion and the ambulance, but never imagining it had to do with us, until Maggie's mother, much later, surged like a fury at us out of the crowd of cheerful fair-goers. Her anger blazed, her eyes lasers, her red hair conflagration. She asked Maggie where her sister was. We said we were looking for her and had been, that she'd wandered off with a friend and friend's mother while we were tossing for goldfish.

Maggie's mother's anger stalled momentarily, a hurricane spinning in place, gaining power, then she swept Maggie away, leaving me standing there, a bagged goldfish in my hand, Maggie's bagged fish lying unbroken on the grass. I picked it up and started a longish walk home. But my mother, already knowing what Maggie and I had not, appeared in her gray Studebaker and picked me up before I crossed Benfield Road. It was from her that I learned about the sister, alive, but with an arm badly broken and perhaps some injury to her head. My mother did not blame me or let me blame myself for the sister's accident, and oddly, for me, I did not feel blame so much as a change I could not name, some combination of a loss of joy, a tacit knowledge that something had ended, a sense of something sad and irreversible.

Maggie, of course, was held to blame by her family long enough that she changed herself dramatically, turning herself almost into a bound girl or a slave to her sister and mother, a martyr taking on a punishment of chores and responsibilities of her own volition. She became permanently sad and shamed, a tall girl now walking always bowed, forgetting how to play. Her change endured through grade school. I saw her rarely out of school because she would not allow herself friends, particularly me. After grade school our paths changed. Now knowing the power of even the most minor of moments to alter us inscrutably and indelibly, I wonder who Maggie became.

That day, my mother drove us home, further down Benfield Road, first between the rows of small brick houses which, we heard tell, had only linoleum floors, then past the larger, statelier homes which stood back behind hedges and were made exotic by an evenly planted tunnel of catalpa trees, cigar trees we called them. These trees were laced with wisteria vines, and in the early summer, the purple wisteria and white catalpa bloomed together, a profusion of Advent, wisteria perfuming the air to intoxication. To get home, we turned right on Riggs Road just before Benfield forked, with Benfield Road going straight and Severna Park Road curving to the left. I will not let myself now imagine the rest of the drive home in terms of what I would see today were I to turn right at Benfield Boulevard.

Severna Park Road travelled past my grade school, over the same train tracks as Benfield Road, and into Severna Park. Immediately over the tracks to the left, white stucco, Gosmann's Grocery. To the right, an old and large dark wood building with a wooden sidewalk out of some western housed a lawyer, a doctor, a real estate office and a dentist who rewarded his young patients with certificates for ice cream cones, something my grandmother found suspicious. I remember most clearly the store I frequented — Doc's, an everything store with a soda and lunch counter, pills and shampoos, tobaccos and pipes and watches, real penny candy bought with real pennies, and a one-armed bandit, even though gambling was against the law in Maryland. One fond memory I have of my grandfather is his holding me up so I could put his nickels in. He'd pull the arm and the fruit would spin. And if we won, we split the nickels, two for me, the rest for him. But nickels went a long way then.

Doc's made phosphates — lime the best. And cherry cokes, lemon cokes, chocolate cokes and brown cows. Grilled cheese with bacon and homemade ice cream, sometimes strawberry or peach, sometimes bing cherry or plum. Doc was a real person with a real wife and as I grew, so did the store and

Severna Park. Eventually, a cement sidewalk extended from in front of Gosmann's and past the Pharmacy where we got prescriptions for coke syrup to treat ailing stomachs, arnica and witch hazel to treat bruises, and paregoric to treat distress of the bowels. Those are the medications I remember most, those and camomile tea and hot lemonade, and once, some blue tablets, miniature coffins, which dissolved in a pan of warm water in which I soaked my foot after I had sliced off a silver dollar sliver of the inside of my heel with the spokes of my bike, riding barefoot and careless. I went home trailing blood. Not the first time nor the last.

If I were, en route to Baltimore from Richmond, to turn right at Benfield Boulevard and follow it to Riggs Road, which no doubt is still the only road out to the peninsula, I know there would be houses everywhere. But — and this is why I always keep on straight up Route 3 into Baltimore — I know that if I did turn right, before I had driven two hundred feet down Benfield Boulevard I would find my inner map erased by multiple lanes and traffic lights, by packs of houses and their necessary strip malls, by professional parks and quick stop shops and Thank God It's Friday restaurants, by crossroads with a gas station or McDonald's in each corner, by diversions from the original road itself. I suspect these diversions exist from a sign indicating that there is Benfield Boulevard and "Old" Benfield Road. If I were to make it to St. Martins-in-the-Field, a field of some expanse surrounded in my time only by thick woods, I am sure I would find the field and woods sold off to more development. Perhaps I would find that the once small and perfectly conical pines that the church assembly bought and planted on the first Arbor Day now shelter, even seclude, the church from the changes in its countryside. But perhaps I would find that they had been razed by some follower of the Fathers Heck and Libby in order to create a new and modern frontage to St. Martin's so that it would stand clear and obvious in its invitation to all who might enter.

No, I will not imagine myself all the way home, a place only in my mind, my heart, my responses to the world always, my memories, occasionally pictures — in the old kayak which rests, full of holes and rips, stranded on the dirt in the half-basement of my current cellar. My home is more within that kayak and amongst the others who have survived and moved along with me than it is in any house or on the river. To actually return might erase my past and thus in some ways erase me.

There are, I think, good reasons to refuse to confront and embrace some of the changes with which life confronts us. The river and the land along it was me, and I was it. I really needed no other companion. It was not that there was no group play — the spontaneous summer evening games when I got caught up in sardines or hide and seek or tag, or the coordinated games we played at school, kickball, dodgeball, red rover, softball, and two games whose names I forget — one played with a ball on tarmac in a square divided into four quadrants, the other with a ball attached to a rope the other end of which was attached to a tall pole. But often that kind of play was, even though I was good at it, perhaps *because* I was good at it, carried out in controlled panic which all too often gave way to pure panic. The world of one group winning over another was not my natural environment, and it often got mean-spirited, particularly when winning involved nothing more important than the many, many things mankind has thought of to do with balls. Yet the pressure was so powerful and real.

The one time at play I remember most is when with some unconscious accuracy, during a game of dodgeball, I swept the ball at my arch rival, red-haired and freckled Mary Sue, and in her rivalry to outmaneuver me, she jumped high, but the ball caught her on her rump and imbalanced her. When the dust cleared, her leg was broken in two places. Sudden reality. But then, in some ways play always leads directly to reality. I instantly became "the one who broke Mary Sue's leg," always the "what's wrong with that girl" girl. That same November day, fifth grade, after Mary Sue had been taken away and we were into the droning hours of afternoon school, Pop Doolin, the old janitor who always struck me as an aged Popeye, broke into our room near collapse, sobs and tears clogging his throat, calling to our teacher, a relentlessly stern woman, "Miz Bay-lus, Miz Bay-lus, the President's done been shot. The President's done been shot." Just before we kids ran without order from the school, because our teachers, shattered and shocked, for a crucial moment forgot our existence, I watched as Mrs. Baylus, tall and stern, shrank and bent and embraced Pop Doolin, shrunken, old and toothless, both weeping and repeating "Oh my God Oh my God." His dark whiskers stood out sharply against his pale, old face.

I ran the length of the deep playground in my green Girl Scout uniform, its skirt restricting my stretched out long-legged run, my knees forcing open seams at the sides of the skirt as they fought its limitations. I ran to where I always met my mother on Girl Scout days, at the corner of Benfield Road and the lane that bordered the back of our school's playground. The only barrier between the back end of our playground and the rest of our world were fat six-foot lengths of creosoted telephone poles, lying evenly spaced along the road where the back of the playground ended. I jumped one, even then, in that moment of stark reality, imagining myself as a horse gone wild. My skirt caught my knee and my front foot did not get high enough. I fell, scrabbled, winded, scraped, and scrambled up and kept on running, veering left to where my mother's car was waiting. Early. It has never surprised me that she would have left to get me early. What has always seemed uncanny was that she and my father always knew exactly where to go to find me. And at the time, thinking myself the bearer of the horrid news, I was surprised when she knew, too, that the president had been shot.

We drove home into a dark week of huddling in my younger sister's bedroom with the black and white television on constantly. There were blankets over the windows because my sister had the *serious* measles. So in that dark room we sat stunned as people filed past the president as he "lay in state," as he lay on his funeral bier.

I would stake a fair amount of money that there is tall fencing around that playground now, that no child can slip down to High's for a snack or take recess on the railroad tracks in exploration, or run home wild from the halls of the school when some disaster strikes. It interests me now, as a teacher, to see how much care is taken of students' hearts and imaginations in school. When there is a tragedy, local or international, there are people trained to come and help quell the fears, to address the dangers of morbid curiosity, to listen as children talk about their negotiations of this or that life explosion. I don't recall anyone ever talking to us about any of the deaths or crises that touched us in those times. No one talked to us about Kennedy, about Audrey, about the heads in the basket, about the several deaths related to fraternity initiations and drownings and collapsing cliffs, about the war in Vietnam. No one talked to us about the Soviet quelling of Czechoslovakians' rebellion for freedom. I had had a pen pal there. It was as if they never knew that we were much aware.

In a way, all these facts seem extraneous, avoidances of the point. Change happens. One must embrace it. But embracing does not require returning as in reunion to detail the change and make those details part of one's memories. I have no need to partake of what has happened to the site of my past since that site was actually mine. My need has been to recover what I can of my past and bring forward in time what I need of it now. And that brings me to the question of the river and what the river means.

A memory: I am thirty-five and fussing with the wiring on my old stereo tuner. My father visits me, clearly depressed. He has been sorting through and purging ancient files and, as he sees it and as I must believe him, discarding his life — throwing out what my mother and I might describe as useless files that date back forty-some years and the half dozen or more jobs that were his stepping stones to retirement. He tells me, "Life is like sticking your thumb in a flowing river. When you die, you remove your thumb and all trace of your life is gone. Most lives are irrelevant." Fussing with wires, an activity I despise, I have two reactions, one to laugh at his use of a thumb in his metaphor, the other to rage at how dismally he dismisses his life, everyday lives. And rage I do, telling him "*Never* say that to me again. It is the lives of everyday people that we need most to honor and understand." My edict seems to make him feel better, but the encounter leaves me chilled and disoriented. I mean, why did I say that to him? What does it mean to him? I ponder his metaphor, for in it, the way he situates himself in terms of *his* river implies that life is something continuous and ongoing and that people wade in then out, birth and death, rather than becoming a part of the river, enlarging the river as it moves endlessly, changing and yet not changing, toward its destination. I realize that I have always situated myself quite differently, more like a bit of matter that enters the river and is after that always a part of the river. If only as a ghost, I will always be part of the Severn, the unexplained small wake rocking a boat on a calm summer evening, the shadow of footprints running thirty feet on an otherwise unmarked beach.

The first time I found myself regularly and consciously connecting back in time to my past was late one night when I was overtired and overworked, teaching eight classes at four different colleges and working full-time on my doctorate at the University of Pennsylvania. What had been random memories and sensations flowed together in a recurring, ever-expanding, sometimes constant yet constantly shifting, collage.

Flashes of memory: sun penetrating clear then murky waters. Buoyancy. Ease. Silence. Days when the waters' temperature is so right that one floats and cannot feel where one's body ends and the river starts. Union. Death. Hunting. Learning. Risk. Fear. Killing. Survival. A day of paddling four miles against high wind and waves and angry current, with every stroke perhaps the last until, almost without expectation, the kayak scrapes up on home shores.

What *can* a river mean? It is more than a place I long to return to, though it is that as well. The motions of crabbing come back to me through all senses, and I see how the act of crabbing has long been one of the metaphors for my life. In my experience, to crab with predictable success demands, in part, trust in what one cannot see and faith in a knowledge that is grounded both in patterns and in lore. To crab with promise also demands, in part, patience, silence, alertness, touch, and steadiness. To crab with success also demands a complexity of coincidences and luck.

When you crab as I crabbed, usually from a twenty-foot wooden canoe, you bait lines, in my case eight of them, with chicken necks and backs and two-ounce lead weights. Then you secure these lines evenly around the canoe — four on one side, four on the other. Then you wait. You watch the lines. In a good dawn there is not much waiting. I remember once catching over four dozen in an hour and calling it quits because I knew we did not need more than that for the family gathering planned that day. My father did not need to go out and buy crabs that day, something we only did when we were hosting a crab feast for extended family. On other days, also good, there is lengthy waiting — sitting in the stern of the canoe, leaning back into the curve of its warm wood, feeling the early morning sun on face and arms and legs, the soft and balmy morning breezes, the rocking of the water soothing. There is never complete silence — the boat and the water slap familiarly at each other; the shores are dotted with occasional people. Boats pass at polite distances, often slowing so as not to rock mine. Gulls and crows shriek and chortle. I am wrapped in a cocoon of hush and peace. I myself am silent, daydreaming and timeless, yet vigilant and alert, poised yet at complete ease. I watch the lines as they move, deciding which is catching a current and which a crab, but there is no haste, no urgency. If a crab gets a good nibble before I pull it in, it deserves it. But I watch the lines as one here, one there, they begin to move away from, sometimes under, the canoe as crabs take ownership of their pieces of chicken. Eventually I stir, but in rhythm with the water and as quiet as the breeze.

I move quietly and lightly toward the tightening line, my net in my right hand. A crab will pull a line as far as it can go and then stay with it, eating. Crabs eats carrion, be it a chicken neck or a victim of drowning. It is their nature. When I reach the line, I silently place the net at an angle so that it rests, invisible from the water, with its head on the crab's side of the canoe and the end of its pole on the gunnel behind me. Then I take the line. At first I take the line slowly with my right index and middle fingers and thumb. I just hold it, no motion, feeling the crab's devouring vibrate up the string. Then I begin, very evenly, very slowly, very gently, to pull the crab toward me. I cannot see it for a good while. I am crabbing in ten to fifteen feet of water, and my lines are at least that long so that they can rest on the bottom. I draw the line up, keeping the slack I create coming into the boat. Drips from the wet string will alert the crab. I do not believe much scares a crab, but they are very cunning and sensitive. I am careful not to drag the line on the edge of the canoe and vibrate a warning down the line to the crab. In pulls of mere inches I smoothly trade the line back and forth between my hands until I begin to see, a scant two feet down, the shape of the bait and the crab. Without pause my left hand takes over the pulling, still slow and incredibly even, wrapping the line around my fingers in a barely perceptible circling. A mere caress of the air. My right hand stretches back to pick up the net. I move it so that the upper part of the rim rests on the gunnels just out of sight from the water. Its wooden shaft sticks out on the other side of the boat. Then, with great evenness and caution, I move the net forward and down gradually into the water, keeping it a few feet from where my left hand is pulling in the crab. Once the net is in the water, I gradually move crab and net towards each other. Sometimes I can pull the crab right into the net, sometimes there is that moment when the crab senses its fate and begins to dart sideways, fast away. Crabs swim very fast. But by then the net and I lean poised at the right distance and angle from the crab and bait. A swift dip and the crab is mine. That last motion is not unlike the strike of a heron or egret. In fact, like the heron and egret, the authentic line crabber is a person of great stillness and waiting, regardless of how great the need. There are other ways to crab, but this is mine, and this patience and timing and focus and connectedness are all part of what the river means.

During periods when I have been out of sync with myself and my life, I have been a bad crabber, jerky and loud, clumsy, impatient. Urgent and angry, I vibrate stress, trip over my feet and tongue, raw senses in chaos. I do not know who I am and I am frightened. I frighten others too, vibrating warnings of dangers down the lines that connect us. In such times, I have been cast out of love because my tension renders me the only one in love. I have been turned away as a friend because I have not been in tune with friendship. I have sat restless and fidgety, giving wrong responses, superficial, making waves, flailing, willing to catch anything, needing without knowing what. But there lives the crabber in me, the innately wise and patient spirit that can sit me down and listen as that crabber says, *Wait. Think. See. Feel. Watch the line. Touch it with a touch that is no touch. Know what you want. Make a fine fit of your space. Quiet. Still. Rock and float. Harmony. One.*

As I get older I find myself more consistently listening to that crabber, returning I hope, to when she and I were, without thought, the same spirit. Listening, becoming, I am more one with my context, more knowing what I want and wanting it honestly and sincerely. Greed and frenzy shed like the skin of a snake. Weighted confusions left behind like the glowing blue tail of a skink, a tail which will decompose where it has fallen, eventually washing down to join some river, while my new tail composes itself. I change. I don't change. I am the sum of all that I remember and all that I do not.